W9-ARL-214

Picture Credits:
Key: b–bottom, t–top, c–center, l–left, r–right

Alamy: 41cr Dinodia Photos, 43l X3A Collection, 72cr David Marchal, 83 Rawf8, 112c Nolan Wynne, 114c mkarco, 116b imageBROKER, 122c Chris Willson, 122b Alfonso de Tomas; **Bibliothèque interuniversitaire de santé, France:** 12bl Bichat; **Getty Images:** 26–27 Digital Vision, 32–33 Viktor Drachev, 92–93 Amelie-Benoist/BSIP, 100–101 Peathegee Inc/Blend Images, 102–103 Echo, 118c Steve Debenport; **LASERPHACO/Dr Patricia Bath:** 98bl; **Library of Congress:** 121bl; **Nanokick Technologies:** 31bl; **NASA:** 104cr; **National Library of Medicine, USA:** 11br; National Museum of American History, USA: 56bl; **National Portrait Gallery, UK:** 62bl; New York Academy of Medicine, USA: 15tl; **Rambam Institute:** 52bl Blaisio Ugolino; **Science Photo Library:** 1 Zephyr, 7cr Christian Darkin, 8–9 John Bavosi, 10–11 Kateryna Kon, 12–13 Innerspace Imaging, 16–17 Gwen Shockey, 18–19 Jacopin/BSIP, 20cr CNX/CNRI, 28b Steve Gschmeissner, 30–31 SGI, 30b Microscape, 38c John Bavosi, 40cl Profs. PM Motta, KR Porter, & PM Andrews, 43br Sheila Terry, 44–45 Amelie-Benoist/BSIP, 46cr KH Fung, 48c Leonello Calvetti, 50–51 KH Fung, 50c Carol & Mike Werner, 52–53 Pixologicstudio, 52cr Steve Gschmeissner, 57 KH Fung, 58–59 Zephyr, 60–61 Francis Leroy, Biocosmos, 62–63 Russell Kightley , 64br Universal History Archive/UIG, 67tr Prof P Motta/Dept of Anatomy/University "La Sapienza", Italy , 75 KH Fung, 75br Steve Gschmeissner, 76tr David M Martin, 77 Springer Medizin, 78–79 Frank Fox, 80–81 KH Fung, 80b Eye of Science, 82cl Anatomical Travelogue, 88cr DO Tromp, 89 Zephyr, 96c Natural History Museum, UK, 100br CNRI, 102cr John Bavosi, 102br Prof P Motta/Dept of Anatomy/University "La Sapienza", Italy, 108c Zephyr, 109tr Prof P Motta/Dept of Anatomy/University "La Sapienza", Italy, 110–111 3D4MEDICAL.COM; **Shutterstock:** Front cover MDGRPHCS, Inside front cover Potapov Alexander, Inside back cover Juan Gaertner, back cover main image and 54–55 Maxisport, 4–5 Masonjar, 4br John Bill, 5tl YanLev, 5c Wallenrock, 5br Monkey Business Images, 6–7 tonkid, 6c theromb, 6bl Georgios Kolidas/C Cook, 7tr BlueRing Media, 8bl Kateryna Kon, 9r Tomacco, 10l Designua, 11cr molekuul_be, 12cl udaix, 13tr Anna Jurkovska, 14–15 Dean Drobot, 14tr racobovt, 15br StevenK, 16cr Orla, 16br Kateryna Kon, 19tl Akif Kutlu, 19cr nicemonkey, 19b Raimundo79, 20–21 Rawpixel.com, 20bl Concretecowb0y, 21b Meletios Verras, 22cr Tong_stocker, 22b Sky Antonio, 23 Nacha Petchdawong, 24–25 Don Mammoser, 24c stockshoppe, 25b Cookie Studio, 26cl kaling2100, 26bl Everett Historical, 27tl udaix, 28cr sciencepics, 29 Potapov Alexander, 31cl Rawpixel.com, 32bl Kjpargeter, 33tl Alex Mit, 33br Designua, 34–35 design36, 34c Artemida–psy, 34bl Everett Historical, 35br Anton Nalivayko, 36–37 oneinchpunch, 36c stihii, 36br Sebastian Kaulitzki, 38bl Lermot, 39cr Irina Bg, 40–41 javarman, 40bl New Vibe, 42cl MriMan, 42c Semnic, 42cr Monet_3k, 42bl Ververidis Vasilis, 44c Okrasyuk, 45cl Dmitry Kalinovsky, 46–47 Alex Brylov, 47cr Designua, 48–49 Merla, 48bl Nadia Buravleva, 49b Alila Medical Media, 50br Arturs Budkevics, 52tr NelaR, 54cr Designua, 55tr Monkey Business Images, 56tr Alila Medical Media, 56cr Quetzalcoatl1, 58l Olga Bolbot, 59tr Tridsanu Thopet, 59bl Neveshkin Nikolay, 60cr Designua, 60c somersault1824, 62cl Timonina, 63c Alila Medical Media, 64c chaiyawat chaidet, 65 Robert Przybysz, 66–67 DavidTB, 66l jacksparrow007, 68–69 Suware Srisomboon, 68tr ifong, 68c overcrew, 70–71 windmoon, 70bl Sebastian Kaulitzki, 71cr metamorworks, 72b Alila Medical Media, 73bl hobbit, 74cr Designua, 74bl elenabsl, 76cr bitt24, 76bl Kateryna Kon, 78b Tefi, 79tr Jose Luis Calvo, 79br Marochkina Anastasiia, 80cr Vasilyeva Larisa, 81tl eranicle, 82cr okili77, 82bl BlueRingMedia, 83tr Life science, 84–85 06photo, 84c Alexey Smolyanyy, 85cr David Cohen 156, 86bl Johan Swanepoel, 87cr sciencepics, 88c Blamb, 88bl Robert Voight, 90–91 MriMan, 90c Vasilisa Tsoy, 91cr Levent Konuk, 92cr Tefi, 92b Juan Gaertner, 94–95 icealex, 94r BlueRingMedia, 95br Kateryna Kon, 96–97 Cipolina, 97b Ermolaev Alexander, 98cr snapgalleria, 98c Peter Hermes Furian, 99 air009, 100cr Alexander_P, 103bl Sakurra, 105 AJP, 105br sihasakprachum, 106–107 WAYHOME studio, 106b BlueRingMedia, 107tl Tero Vesalainen, 107bl a katz, 108–109 medistock, 108cr Tefi, 108bl Timonina, 110ct Romaset, 110cb john dory, 110bl Semmick Photo, 111tl GagliardiImages, 112–113 Fakhrul Najmi, 112b Alila Medical Media, 113b Stefan Dinse, 114–115 Olesia Bilkei, 115cr michaeljung, 116–117 Rawpixel.com, 116c tammykayphoto, 118–119 Rob Crandall, 118bl Macrovector, 119tr Dean Drobot, 120–121 Rawpixel.com, 120cr IVASHstudio, 120b Monkey Business Images, 122–123 Yavuz Sariyildiz, 123bl Macrovector, 124–125 Zdenka Darula, 124c Tsomka, 124bl Maquiladora, 125cr Sonpichit Salangsing; **US Information Agency:** 17tl; **Wellcome Images:** 23tl, 29tl, 44bl, 54bl, 71tl, 79tl, 87tl, 94bl; **Wikimedia Commons:** 24bl DBCLS/BodyParts3D, 37bl Advanced Microscopy Group/paultmoon, 46bl MSM Takrouri & M Khalaf, 51tl J Solis Cohen, 60bl Popular Science Monthly (vol. 58), 65bl Biographical Memoirs of the National Academy of Sciences (vol. 40), 67bl Journal of Chemical Education, 68bl Wielka Encyklopedia Powszechna PWN, 90bl Mark Dow, Brain Development Lab, University of Oregon, USA, 93bl Clark University/Garrondo, 96bl DBCLS/BodyParts3D, 101tl Joe Haupt, 104bl, 114bl, 117tl Sarah–Jayne Blakemore, UCL/Shamus O'Reilly.

ARCTURUS

This edition published in 2018 by Arcturus Publishing Limited
26/27 Bickels Yard, 151–153 Bermondsey Street,
London SE1 3HA

Copyright © Arcturus Holdings Limited

In this book, one billion means one thousand million (1,000,000,000) and one trillion means one million million (1,000,000,000,000).

All rights reserved. No part of this publication may be reproduced, stored in a retrieval system, or transmitted, in any form or by any means, electronic, mechanical, photocopying, recording or otherwise, without prior written permission in accordance with the provisions of the Copyright Act 1956 (as amended). Any person or persons who do any unauthorised act in relation to this publication may be liable to criminal prosecution and civil claims for damages.

Consultant: Dr Mandy Hartley
Author and Editor: Clare Hibbert @ Hollow Pond
Designer: Amy McSimpson @ Hollow Pond

ISBN: 978-1-78828-610-7
CH006258US
Supplier 29, Date 1018, Print run 7985

Printed in China

CHILDREN'S ENCYCLOPEDIA OF THE HUMAN BODY

CONTENTS

Introduction

Great thinkers have argued for thousands of years about what humans are. Like all animals, we have an amazing body that has evolved over time. We also have special abilities that make us stand out from other animals.

Worldwide Family

Today there are more than seven billion humans on Earth. We belong to one species but we don't all look the same. Over thousands of years our bodies slowly adapted to suit different environments, because humans with useful characteristics were most likely to survive and reproduce. This process is called natural selection.

Black or white, tall or short, skinny or plump ... we're diverse but we belong to one species, *Homo sapiens*.

In the Animal Kingdom

Scientists organize living things into groups with shared characteristics. Our body has a backbone, so we are vertebrates. We breathe air, have hair, and feed our babies, so we are mammals. Our intelligence, flexible fingers and toes, fingernails, and forward-facing eyes place us with the primates. Being large and tailless makes us great apes.

Humans need more looking after than most mammal babies. Foals walk minutes after they're born, but humans cannot do that for months.

Super Senses

Our understanding of the world around us comes from our senses of sight, hearing, smell, taste, and touch. Extra senses make us aware of hot and cold, pain, balance and gravity, and where our body is in relation to everything else. Our brain uses all this sense data to respond usefully to our surroundings.

This spearfisher relies on senses to know where his limbs are, find a fish, and fire his spear accurately.

Hands Free

Humans are the only primates that walk upright all the time. This frees up our hands to use tools, carry things, and communicate with each other by drawing, writing, and even texting.

Our fingers and thumbs work together so we can hold things precisely.

Cleverness

Human intelligence is driven by the brain's processing power. We can solve problems, plan ahead, learn and remember, feel emotions, and much more. Other animals show some of these mental abilities—but even the cleverest ones don't match humans in all these areas.

Sharing books is one way humans pass on knowledge.

Body Chemistry

The body is a collection of complex systems of organs and tissues which, in turn, are made of cells. Like all matter, cells are built from basic substances called elements. An element is a chemical that contains only one type of atom. Nearly half of the 118 known elements are found in the body.

Elementary Ingredients

Most elements in the body are "trace elements"—we have only a tiny trace of them. They include metals such as magnesium (0.05 percent), iron (0.006 percent), zinc (0.0032 percent), and copper (0.0001 percent).

An adult should drink at least six to eight glasses of water a day—more if he or she is very active.

TRACE ELEMENTS (3.8 %)
Trace elements include calcium (1.5 %), essential for healthy bones and teeth, and phosphorus (1 %), which provides energy in cells for chemical reactions.

HYDROGEN (9.5 %)
Hydrogen (9.5 percent) is found in water and all organic molecules (lipids, proteins, carbohydrates, and nucleic acids).

NITROGEN (3.2 %)
Nitrogen is found in proteins, used for nearly every process in a cell, and in the nucleic acids that make up DNA.

OXYGEN (65 %)
Oxygen is mostly in the form of water. One oxygen atom (O) bonded to two hydrogen atoms (H_2) forms a molecule of water (H_2O).

CARBON (18.5 %)
Carbon is found in all organic molecules.

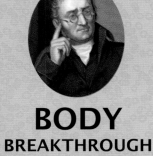

BODY BREAKTHROUGH

Scientist: John Dalton
Breakthrough: Theory of atoms
Date: 1803
The story: Dalton said that everything is made of atoms, that atoms are indivisible and indestructible, and that all atoms of a given element have the same properties. Dalton observed that a combination of two or more kinds of atom (such as oxygen and hydrogen) can form a compound (in that case, water).

An adult's body weight is 55–60 percent water. Water is the base ingredient of blood, urine, and all other bodily fluids.

This diagram shows one atom of carbon. Having four electrons in its outer shell means it can form many types of bonds with other atoms.

Basic Building Block

Many molecules in living organisms contain carbon. The structure of a carbon atom allows it to bond with various elements to form stable molecules. It bonds with hydrogen and oxygen to form carbohydrates and lipids (fatty acids); with hydrogen, oxygen, and nitrogen to form proteins; and with hydrogen, oxygen, nitrogen, and phosphorus to form nucleic acids.

The only life forms we know are carbon-based. This artwork imagines a world where creatures are built from crystals of silicon, an element that can cope with very high temperatures.

DID YOU KNOW? More than 96 percent of the body is made up of just four elements—oxygen, carbon, hydrogen, and nitrogen.

Cells

Scientists cannot be sure exactly how many cells the body contains, but they estimate that there around 37.2 trillion! Cells are the tiny structures that are the basic unit of all living organisms.

Parts of the Cell

Most cells can only be seen through a microscope, but they are incredibly complex. They contain chemical machines called organelles that carry out different jobs.

INSIDE A HUMAN CELL

1. Nucleus contains the body's DNA.
2. Pore-pitted nuclear membrane
3. Nucleolus makes the substances that build ribosomes.
4. Endoplasmic reticulum makes and stores proteins.
5. Mitochondrion fuels the cell by releasing energy from sugars, starch, proteins, and fats.
6. Golgi apparatus stores substances or gets them ready to leave the cell.
7. Ribosomes build proteins (see pages 18-19).
8. Perixosomes break down toxins, amino acids, and lipids (fatty acids).
9. Lyosomes break down waste.
10. Centrioles help the cell divide.
11. Cytoplasm is a jelly-like fluid.
12. Cell membrane protects the cell.
13. Pore, where some molecules can enter or leave the cell

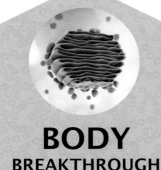

BODY
BREAKTHROUGH

Scientist: Camillo Golgi
Breakthrough: Identified the golgi apparatus
Date: 1898
The story: Italian scientist Camillo Golgi invented a technique for staining cells black so that he could examine neurons under a microscope. The staining revealed a stack of "disks" inside the cell—the organelle we now call the golgi apparatus. Golgi was later awarded a Nobel Prize for his work on the brain.

DID YOU KNOW? Animals, plants, and fungi are built from eukaryotic cells—cells that have a nucleus enclosed in a membrane. Prokaryotic cells don't have this.

Specialist Jobs

We have hundreds of types of cell, each suited to a particular function. Epithelial cells, for example, line surfaces of the body, such as the skin, vessels, or organs. Depending on the job they do, they can be flat, cube-shaped, column-shaped, or column-shaped with hairs on top.

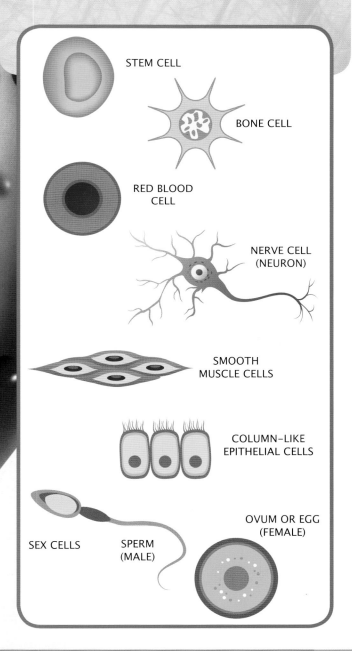

STEM CELL

BONE CELL

RED BLOOD CELL

NERVE CELL (NEURON)

SMOOTH MUSCLE CELLS

COLUMN–LIKE EPITHELIAL CELLS

SEX CELLS   SPERM (MALE)   OVUM OR EGG (FEMALE)

An average cell is 0.025 mm (0.001 in) across. The largest, an ovum (egg cell), is about the size of a full stop.

How Cells Divide

The body produces new cells so that we can grow, and also to replace cells that are damaged or dying. Cells have different lifespans. Some white blood cells survive for just a few hours, while the epithelial cells that line the gut last about five days. The lens of the eye lasts a lifetime.

Copy That!

Most new body cells are made in a process called mitosis, which produces exact copies of genetic material. Sex cells (page 108) are the exception. They need to make "half" (not full) copies so they use a different method, called meiosis.

Each daughter cell will have its own membrane and be filled with jelly-like fluid called cytoplasm.

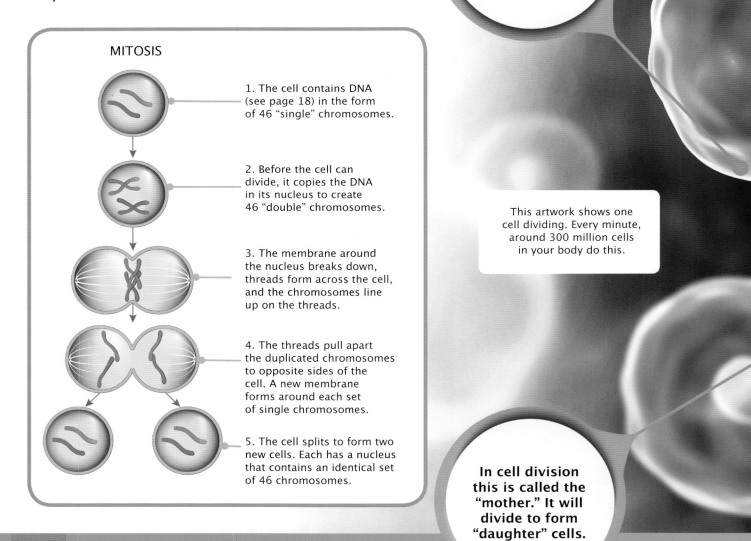

MITOSIS

1. The cell contains DNA (see page 18) in the form of 46 "single" chromosomes.

2. Before the cell can divide, it copies the DNA in its nucleus to create 46 "double" chromosomes.

3. The membrane around the nucleus breaks down, threads form across the cell, and the chromosomes line up on the threads.

4. The threads pull apart the duplicated chromosomes to opposite sides of the cell. A new membrane forms around each set of single chromosomes.

5. The cell splits to form two new cells. Each has a nucleus that contains an identical set of 46 chromosomes.

This artwork shows one cell dividing. Every minute, around 300 million cells in your body do this.

In cell division this is called the "mother." It will divide to form "daughter" cells.

Each daughter cell is an exact copy of its mother, with all the DNA in its nucleus.

Powerful Proteins

Cells contain substances called proteins. Some proteins, such as collagen, help to give the cell its structure. Others, known as enzymes, carry out chemical reactions inside the cell. There are also proteins that transport signals or atoms within cells or between them.

Collagen molecules twist together in threes. The resulting triple chains are long and strong.

Scientist: Walther Flemming
Breakthrough: Mitosis
Date: 1878
The story: German biologist Walther Flemming studied salamander cells and how they divided. He noticed that thread-like structures (chromosomes) were shared between the two new cells (but not that they were exact copies). Flemming called the cell division process *mitosis*, from the Greek word for "thread."

BODY
BREAKTHROUGH

DID YOU KNOW? Every minute we lose 30,000–40,000 cells from the epidermis (surface of our skin) … but we also produce 30,000–40,000 replacements.

Tissues

Cells are fragile on their own, but not when they join together to form tissue. The four main types are muscle, epithelial, connective, and nervous tissue. All tissues need a blood supply to deliver nutrients. Most also have nerve fibers that allow them to feel pain.

Tissue Functions

Muscle tissue lets us move or keep still. Epithelial tissue lines and protects our organs. Connective tissue, such as bone, cartilage, fat, and blood, holds other tissues together and protects them. Nervous tissue is made up of neurons, which carry messages between cells, and glial cells, which carry nutrients and oxygen to the neurons.

This SEM—an image from a scanning electron microscope—reveals the tissues that make up the lining of the jejunum (part of the small intestine).

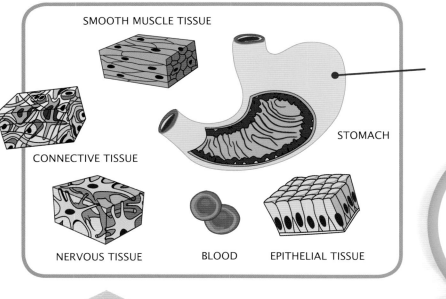

SMOOTH MUSCLE TISSUE

CONNECTIVE TISSUE

STOMACH

NERVOUS TISSUE

BLOOD

EPITHELIAL TISSUE

In an organ, several types of tissue work together. The stomach contains smooth muscle, epithelial, connective, nervous, and blood tissue.

The mucus membrane is formed from epithelial tissue. It houses glands and cells that secrete mucus.

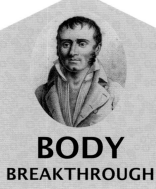

BODY BREAKTHROUGH

Scientist: Marie-François-Xavier Bichat
Breakthrough: Founded histology (the science of studying tissues)
Date: 1800
The story: French anatomist Marie-François-Xavier Bichat was one of the first to suggest that organs are formed from simple tissues that each had different functions. His *Treatise on Membranes* (1800) identified 21 types of tissue. However, Bichat didn't use a microscope so he didn't see that tissues are made up of cells.

DID YOU KNOW? Tissues also contain a non-living ingredient, called the intercellular matrix, which fills the spaces between the cells.

Liquid Tissue

Blood (see pages 60–61) counts as a type of tissue because it is made up of different types of cell working together. Its many functions include transporting nutrients and waste substances, and helping to keep our temperature steady.

Blood tissue is inside vessels, seen here under a microscope. The vessels' walls are built from smooth and connective muscle.

A sheet of smooth muscle tissue squeezes digested food along the small intestine.

A layer of connective tissue nourishes the epithelial tissue and fixes it to the muscle tissue.

Organs

Any working part of the body machine that is made from more than one type of tissue is an organ. We have 78 organs, but only a handful are essential to our survival. The five vital organs are the brain, heart, lungs, kidneys, and liver.

Big Five

The brain controls the other organs. The heart pumps the blood, carrying oxygen taken in by the lungs. The kidneys remove waste from the blood, while the liver filters out harmful substances and produces proteins that help our blood to clot and bile, which helps to break down fats.

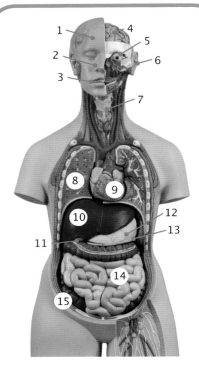

KEY TO ORGANS

1. Skin	9. Heart
2. Nose	10. Liver
3. Mouth	11. Gall bladder
4. Brain	12. Stomach
5. Eye	13. Pancreas
6. Ear	14. Small intestine
7. Larynx	15. Large intestine
8. Lungs	

This torso, used to teach anatomy, shows some of the body's organs.

The brain is the most complex organ in the body. It controls everything else.

The nose is an organ used for breathing and smelling. It plays a part in both the respiratory and sensory systems.

DID YOU KNOW? The liver is the heaviest internal organ. The average weight of an adult's liver is 1.6 kg (3.5 lb).

Pioneers: Ancient Egyptians
Breakthrough: First description of the body's organs
Date: *c.* 1600 BCE
The story: The Edwin Smith Papyrus, named after the American Egyptologist who bought it in 1862, is one of the four main medical works known from ancient Egypt. It gives treatments for 48 different injuries, which have been grouped together according to the organs they affect. It shows that the Egyptians studied the body scientifically.

The skin stops water and microbes entering the body. It is also a habitat for around 1,000 harmless bacteria species.

The brain controls the swimmer's muscles and movement. The lungs bring in oxygen, while the heart pumps blood.

The Biggest Organ

Weighing around 4.5 kg (10 lb) on an average adult, the skin is the body's biggest organ. It is one of the external organs, visible outside the body. Others include the eyes, tongue, and penis. Internal organs are inside the body.

On an average adult, the skin covers an area of about 1.8 sq m (22 sq ft).

Body Systems

Like cells and tissues, organs don't work alone. They join up with other organs and tissues to form body systems. Each system performs one function or set of functions, such as digestion or breathing.

Fully Functional

The body's systems need each other in order to work properly. They rely on the nervous and endocrine systems to control what they do, and when. They also need the circulatory system to bring oxygen that has been breathed in and energy from food that has been digested.

Muscles are organs made of muscle tissue, blood vessels, tendons, and nerves. They form the muscular system, which works with the skeletal system so we can move.

RESPIRATORY SYSTEM

ENDOCRINE AND EXOCRINE SYSTEM

DIGESTIVE SYSTEM

The thyroid gland secretes hormones that keep the body's temperature, metabolism, and heart rate steady.

Home of the Hormones

The endocrine system has glands that make chemical messengers called hormones. Each hormone triggers a different action—for example, adrenaline prepares the body for action, by increasing our heart rate and our rate of breathing.

The digestive system processes food. It includes the esophagus, stomach, and intestine.

BODY
BREAKTHROUGH

Scientists: Rosalyn Sussman Yalow (left) and Solomon Berson
Breakthrough: Discovered radioimmunoassay (RIA)
Date: 1977
The story: Using forms of elements called isotopes, RIA makes it possible to measure very accurately substances that were previously very hard to measure or even too small to detect. Yalow and Berson first used RIA to measure insulin levels and, later, many other hormones. Another plus is that RIA is an inexpensive method of testing.

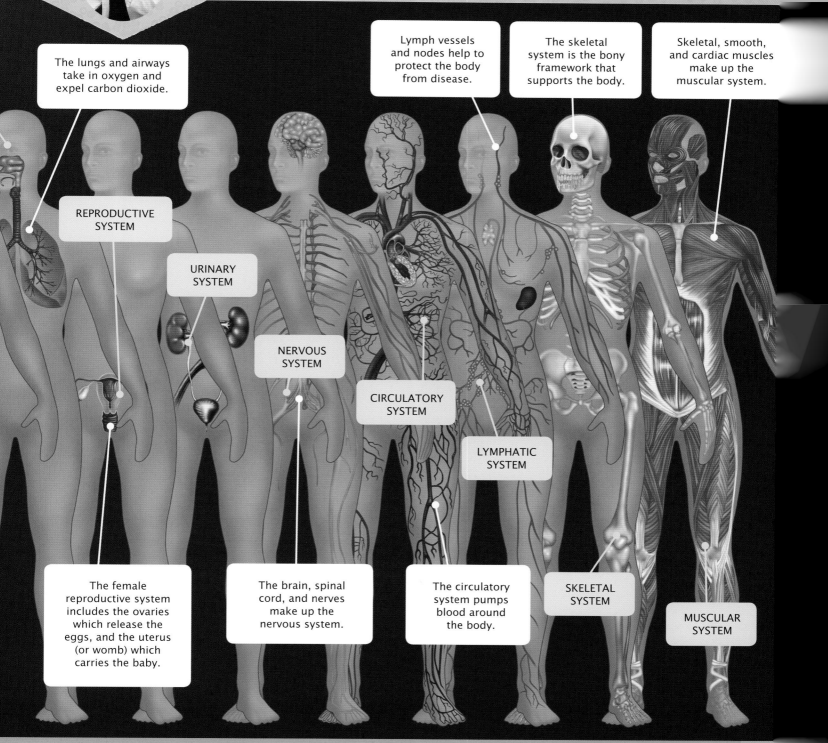

The lungs and airways take in oxygen and expel carbon dioxide.

Lymph vessels and nodes help to protect the body from disease.

The skeletal system is the bony framework that supports the body.

Skeletal, smooth, and cardiac muscles make up the muscular system.

REPRODUCTIVE SYSTEM

URINARY SYSTEM

NERVOUS SYSTEM

CIRCULATORY SYSTEM

LYMPHATIC SYSTEM

The female reproductive system includes the ovaries which release the eggs, and the uterus (or womb) which carries the baby.

The brain, spinal cord, and nerves make up the nervous system.

The circulatory system pumps blood around the body.

SKELETAL SYSTEM

MUSCULAR SYSTEM

DID YOU KNOW? The pea-sized pituitary gland may be small, but it releases many hormones—which control our blood pressure and our growth, for example.

Genes and DNA

Genes are instructions that decide how cells look and what they do. They perform that task by building proteins—vitally important substances for life. Genes are stored in the nucleus of every cell on a long, twisting molecule called DNA. Another type of molecule called RNA (ribonucleic acid) acts as a messenger, carrying the DNA's instructions out of the nucleus.

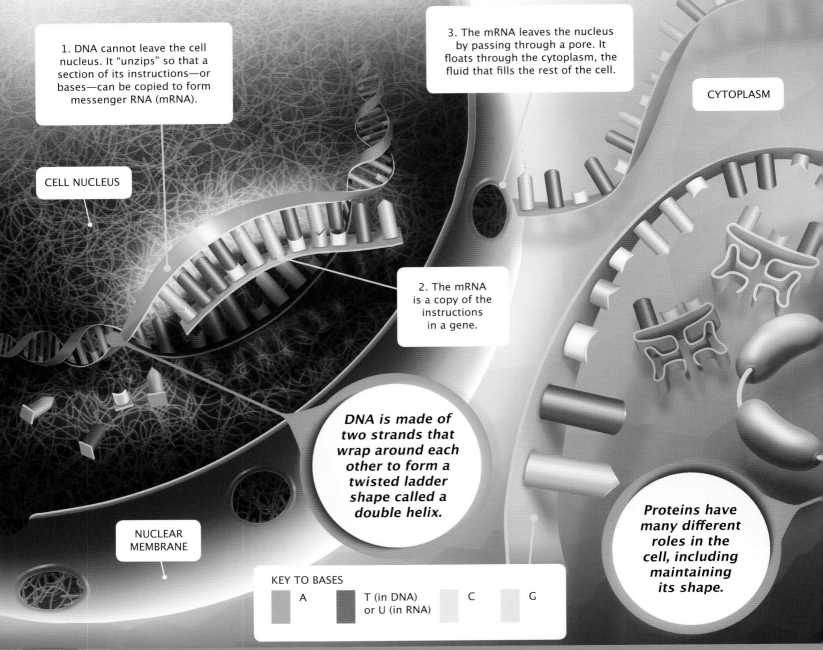

1. DNA cannot leave the cell nucleus. It "unzips" so that a section of its instructions—or bases—can be copied to form messenger RNA (mRNA).

3. The mRNA leaves the nucleus by passing through a pore. It floats through the cytoplasm, the fluid that fills the rest of the cell.

CYTOPLASM

CELL NUCLEUS

2. The mRNA is a copy of the instructions in a gene.

DNA is made of two strands that wrap around each other to form a twisted ladder shape called a double helix.

Proteins have many different roles in the cell, including maintaining its shape.

NUCLEAR MEMBRANE

KEY TO BASES

A   T (in DNA) or U (in RNA)   C   G

DID YOU KNOW? The human body has 20,000–25,000 genes. Each gene has a start and stop point, and is made up of combinations of As, Cs, Gs, and Ts.

BODY BREAKTHROUGH

Scientists: Francis Crick, James Watson, Rosalind Franklin, and Maurice Wilkins
Breakthrough: DNA's double helix structure
Date: 1953
The story: Francis Crick and James Watson used data gathered by fellow scientists Rosalind Franklin and Maurice Wilkins to work out the shape of the DNA molecule. They showed it formed a double helix, like a twisted ladder, with "rungs" of chemicals called bases.

Bases

If you imagine DNA as a language, then its "letters" are bases. DNA has just four chemical bases: adenine (A), thymine (T), cytosine (C), and guanine (G). In double-stranded DNA, A always bonds with T and C with G.

These bands show the bases in a DNA sequence.

4. The cytoplasm contains many different organelles, including ribosomes, the cell's protein–building "machines."

tRNA

5. Ribosomes allow mRNA to connect to another molecule, tRNA. Each tRNA carries a simple compound called an amino acid.

AMINO ACID

Building from Bases

If bases are "letters" in the genetic code of DNA and RNA, then its "words" are codons, which are three bases long. Each codon provides the key to build a particular amino acid—the building blocks of proteins. Every protein is made from the same 20 amino acids.

6. As mRNA and tRNA connect, chains of amino acids link together, forming proteins. Proteins play many different roles in the cell. They are sometimes called the cell's "workers."

This model shows a molecule of hemoglobin, the protein that makes red blood cells red. Each colored structure is a different amino acid.

Inherited Characteristics

Half of our genes come from our mother and half from our father. Since genes are the instructions that build the body, it's no surprise that we "take after" our parents. The genetic code we inherit decides the texture of our hair, how well we can see, the strength of our teeth, and much more.

In Control

A chromosome is a long, thread-like structure made of a coiled-up molecule of DNA and some proteins. All 46 of our chromosomes (23 pairs) are in every cell that has a nucleus. The last pair, the sex chromosomes, make us male or female.

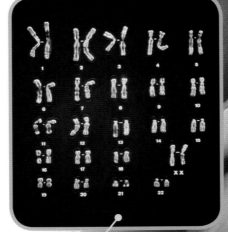

This micrograph shows all 23 pairs of chromosomes. Here, the last pair are XX (female). In men, the sex chromosomes are XY.

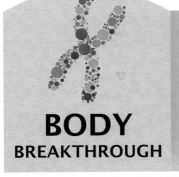

BODY
BREAKTHROUGH

Pioneers: Human Genome Project (HGP)
Breakthrough: Sequenced the human genome
Date: 2003
The story: Beginning in 1990, the HGP set out to map the human genome—to record the order of the 3.2 billion pairs of chemical bases (A, T, C, and G) that spell out the genetic code on our 23 chromosomes. The project took 13 years. Today, its findings are accessible to scientists all over the world.

DID YOU KNOW? The HGP's first director was James Watson, the scientist who had co-discovered the double helix structure of DNA.

Genes don't only affect how we look. They also contribute to our mental state and the way we behave.

Characteristics such as what we eat and how much we sleep are determined by a mix of genes and other non-genetic factors.

Curing Disease

Scientists hope to wipe out inherited diseases by "editing" genes—adding, taking away, or altering faulty bits—but it won't be easy. Most cases of inherited breast cancer are linked to mutations in two genes, BRCA1 and BRCA2, but there may be as many as 20 other genes that increase our risk of breast cancer.

CRISPR-Cas9

CRISPR-Cas9 is new technology that allows scientists to precisely remove, add, or alter faulty sections of genes.

The Conscious Mind

The building blocks of the human body are very similar to those of other animals. But we're different to animals—we're not simply a body, we also have a mind. Humans can learn, remember, plan, and act in a unique way, which we call consciousness. So what is the mind made of?

Mind and Brain

Many scientists believe that understanding how the brain works will answer all the questions we have about how consciousness is made. They can map which parts of the brain we use for different types of conscious activity (see pages 90–91).

Nature and Nurture

The mind functions only when the brain is working, so it depends on the brain we're born with ("nature"). Outside influences ("nurture") such as diet and learning also affect how the brain develops. So the mind is built from a mix of nature and nurture.

This performer's drawn-on frown is a symbol. Our ability to use symbols is part of being conscious.

Many people believe our consciousness is part of a spiritual force that exists beyond us. We might use meditation or other rituals to connect to this spiritual force.

Having a mind lets us overcome our natural fears. We can enjoy the thrill of activities such as skydiving.

Part of self-awareness is knowing that we are looking at ourself when we see our reflection in the mirror.

Scientist: Melanie Klein
Breakthrough: Play therapy
Date: 1932
The story: Melanie Klein was trained by fellow Austrian Sigmund Freud, founder of psychoanalysis. Psychoanalysts treat mental illness by finding the fears that lurk in a patient's unconscious mind. Children are too young for the usual "talking therapy," so Klein developed play therapy, a method still used to help children make sense of how they feel, think, and behave.

Humans love storytelling. Our minds organize information into stories, in which one event causes the next.

DID YOU KNOW? Dreams can help us to understand connections and memories in our unconscious—the part of the mind we can't really access.

Language and Communication

Humans use many tools to share ideas and feelings, so we can live and work together. We communicate with our bodies and our facial expressions. We also learn a language from our community that helps us to think, and to swap ideas and stories. Our ability to use language is a big part of who we are.

Making Words

Humans make precise sounds, called phonemes, to build words and sentences. We use our teeth, tongue, breath, and larynx (voicebox) to make phonemes, just like we use our fingers to write or type the letters of an alphabet.

Our breath passes through the voicebox in the throat. If our vocal cords are open and relaxed, we are silent. If they stretch tight, the breath makes them vibrate and produce sound.

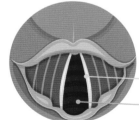
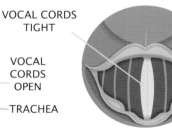

VOCAL CORDS
TIGHT

VOCAL
CORDS
OPEN

TRACHEA

Breathing silently

Making a sound

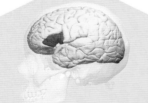

BODY
BREAKTHROUGH

Scientist: Paul Broca
Breakthrough: Discovered Broca's area
Date: 1861
The story: French surgeon Paul Broca found that two patients who couldn't speak had damage in the same area of their brain. This was the first scientific evidence for the idea that each human ability happens in a specific part of the brain. His theory helped to launch brain science.

DID YOU KNOW? After two million responses, testyourvocab.com found that the average eight-year-old already knows 10,000 words.

Some body language may be special to our culture, and some is shared by all humans.

Body language is not just gestures. It is also how we position our body in relation to others.

We interpret not just the words in speech, but also the pitch changes that convey meaning and emotion.

Body Language

Some scientists argue that most of what we "say" is not through words—it's the messages we send and receive through body movements. We can certainly use words to communicate over distance or time. But to connect fully with each other, we often prefer to be together.

Body language can be "closed" or "open." Crossed arms or legs may communicate that we are holding back.

Body language can show what a speaker isn't telling us—and even reveal if they're lying.

The Skeleton

Humans are vertebrates—we have a backbone or spine made up of linked bones called vertebrae. All the other bones in the body join directly or indirectly to the spine, from our tiny ear bones to our femur (thighbone). Together, they form the skeleton.

Jobs for the Bones

The skeleton gives the body shape and support. The bones that make up the central (axial) skeleton—skull bones, spine, ribs, and breastbone (sternum)—protect our vital organs. The attached (appendicular) skeleton—arms, hands, legs, feet, shoulder blades, and pelvis—allow us to move.

The upper arm bone is called the humerus. It runs from the shoulder to the elbow.

This X-ray shows the pelvis, which supports the upper body, links the legs to the spine, and shields the bladder, reproductive organs, and bowel. It is made up of the hip bones (1), sacrum (2), and coccyx (3).

The "funny bone" isn't a bone—it's a nerve! If we bump it at the elbow, it really hurts.

BODY
BREAKTHROUGH

Scientist: Wilhelm Röntgen
Breakthrough: First X-rays of the human skeleton
Date: 1895
The story: German physicist Wilhelm Röntgen discovered X-rays by accident. These rays couldn't pass through certain solids. Röntgen realized X-rays allowed doctors to view bones without cutting open the body. The first X-ray was of his wife's hand. Röntgen won the Nobel Prize for his discovery.

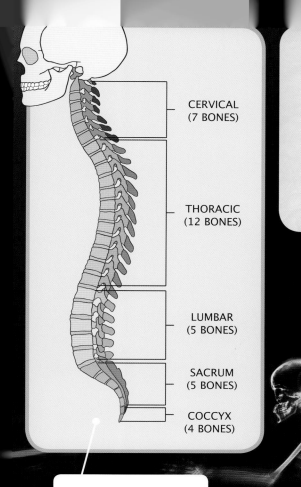

CERVICAL
(7 BONES)

THORACIC
(12 BONES)

LUMBAR
(5 BONES)

SACRUM
(5 BONES)

COCCYX
(4 BONES)

Naturally Curved

There are three main types of vertebrae: cervical, which support the head and neck and let them move; thoracic, attached to the ribs; and lumbar, supporting the upper body. Beneath these, at the base of the spine, are the wedge-shaped sacrum and tail-like coccyx.

Like a bony crash helmet, the skull protects the delicate, vulnerable brain.

In adults, the sacrum and coccyx have become sections of fused vertebrae.

Both men and women have 12 pairs of curved ribs. These bones form a cage around the heart and lungs.

The way our bones are joined together gives us the flexibility to move. We can run, jump, climb, and more.

DID YOU KNOW? An adult has 206 individual bones. There are 80 in the central skeleton; the other 126 make up the attached skeleton.

Our Bones

Bones look solid, but only the outer layer is hard and compact. Their core is light and spongy, made of living tissue. This structure means that bones are strong but incredibly light—an average person's skeleton weighs only around 10 kg (22 lb).

Types of Bone

The five bone types are short, long, flat, sesamoid, and irregular. Short bones, such as the carpals in the wrist, are as wide as they are long. Long bones, such as the leg bones, are longer than they are wide. Flat bones are plate-like and include the breastbone (sternum) and bones of the pelvis. The kneecap is one of the sesamoid bones—small, round bones found within tendons. Irregular bones, such as the hyoid bone in the neck, don't fit any of the other groups.

NERVE

This long bone has a thin coating of connective tissue over a layer of compact bone. Next is a layer of spongy bone and a central canal of soft bone marrow and blood vessels.

BONE MARROW

BLOOD VESSELS

SPONGY BONE

COMPACT BONE

MEMBRANE

Bone Marrow

Bones contain soft, jelly-like tissue called marrow. Red bone marrow produces blood cells and is found in all of a baby's bones. Over time some of it is replaced with yellow marrow, which makes fat, cartilage, and bone. Adults keep red marrow in the skull, spine, sternum, ribs, shoulder, hip bones, and ends of long bones.

This SEM scan shows the honeycomb structure of spongy bone. Its bone marrow (shown in blue) is making blood cells (pink).

The top teeth are held by two bones called the maxillae, which are fused to the cheek bones.

Scientist: Mansur ibn Ilyas
Breakthrough: First illustrated atlas of the human body
Date: *c.* 1390
The story: Persian scholar Mansur ibn Ilyas divided his atlas of the human body into five chapters: bones, nerves, muscles, veins, and arteries. The section on bones included small diagrams of the joins where (in adults) the skull bones have fused together.

The facial skeleton has 14 irregular bones in a variety of shapes and sizes. The top of the skull is formed from eight bones.

Eight large, curved bones surround and protect the brain.

The mandible is the only bone in the skull that can move. It holds the bottom row of teeth and joins the cranial vault at the ears.

DID YOU KNOW? The face is symmetrical because all its bones, apart from the mandible and vomer (the bone between the nostrils), are in pairs.

How Bones Grow

By the time you are 20 years old, the bones in your hand will have grown and the joints will have closed.

Bones are made up of calcium, phosphorus, sodium, and other minerals. They also contain collagen (the protein that gives tissues in the body their strength and stretchiness). Using these ingredients, our body can build bones so that we can grow into fully formed adults and mend bones that fracture (break).

Lengthy Process

Bone grows from a soft, rubbery substance called cartilage. Inside the cartilage, small lumps of bone develop. These are called ossification centers—*ossification* means "hardening of a soft tissue into bone." As these areas spread, our cartilage becomes bone, and our bones grow longer.

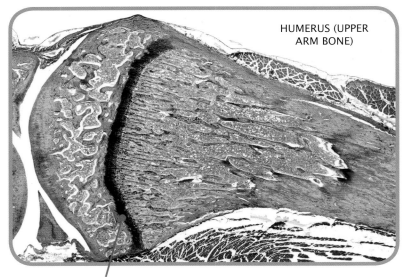

HUMERUS (UPPER ARM BONE)

Each end of a long bone has a growth plate (dark blue in this SEM scan), where new cartilage cells form.

The palm is made of five bones called metacarpels.

Each finger has three finger bones (phalanges). The thumb has two.

DID YOU KNOW? Over half of us break a bone before the age of 18. The most common childhood fractures are to the wrist, elbow, fingers, or collarbone.

Bone Repair

Some fractures break the bone completely, while others just make a crack in the bone. However serious the break, blood seeps into the space to form a clot. Then a thick patch of cartilage called a callus forms around the clot. Over time, this cartilage turns to bone (ossifies).

At three years old, only a few of the eight carpels (wrist bones) have formed.

The doctor lines up the broken limbs so that they will mend in the right positions. Supports called casts hold the bones in place while they are healing.

This X-ray shows bone as greeny-yellow and cartilage and flesh as red and purple.

The joints between the finger bones have cartilage where bone will form and grow.

BODY
BREAKTHROUGH

Scientists: Professors Matthew Dalby and Stuart Reid, and their team at the University of Glasgow, Scotland

Breakthrough: Used nanotechnology to make artificial bone

Date: 2017

The story: Matthew Dalby, Stuart Reid, and team used a technique called nanokicking—hitting cells with very precise, faint vibrations—to grow human bone. Nanokicking stem cells in collagen turned the collagen into synthetic bone or "bone putty."

Joints

Our body has about 400 joints—places where bones meet. Some joints are fixed; others are semi-movable (for example, the tough pads of cartilage between the vertebrae don't allow much movement). However, most joints move freely. The shapes of the bone ends decide how much mobility each joint has.

Types of Movable Joint

At pivot joints, one bone rotates in a collar formed by another bone. In saddle joints, one bone "sits" on the other, like a rider on a horse. Hinge joints simply bend and straighten. At plane joints, flat bones slide over each other, back and forth or sideways. Ellipsoidal joints are where a rounded bone fits into a cavity. Ball-and-socket joints, where a round bone end fits a "cup," are the most mobile.

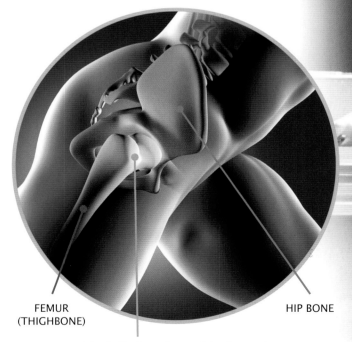

FEMUR (THIGHBONE)

HIP BONE

The ball-shaped top of the femur fits into a rounded socket in the hip bone. This gives a big range of movement: up and down, back and forth, and rotating around.

Circus acrobats are sometimes called "double-jointed." They don't really have more joints—they just have more flexible ones.

The shoulder joint is one of the most mobile joints in the body.

DID YOU KNOW? In adults, the skull bones have fixed joints. Connective tissue called sutures has knitted them together so they can't move.

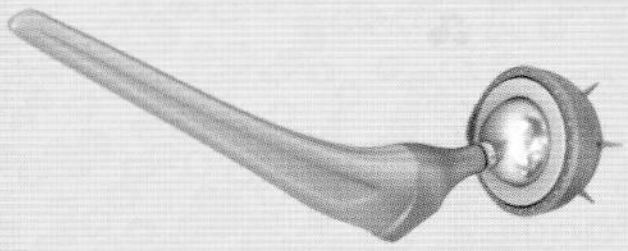

Scientist: John Charnley
Breakthrough: Developed total hip replacement surgery
Date: 1962
The story: Early hip replacements were painful, didn't allow much movement, and sometimes even squeaked! British orthopedic surgeon John Charnley designed an artificial hip joint with a low-friction coating on the socket so that the femur could move freely. Its design, and Charnley's surgical technique, are still used today.

The wrist is an ellipsoidal joint. The rounded ends of two of the carpal bones fits into an oval cavity at the end of the radius (a lower arm bone).

FEMUR

SYNOVIAL FLUID

PATELLA

CARTILAGE

TIBIA

Slippy Liquid

At movable joints, the bone ends are covered in a layer of smooth cartilage. They are also bathed in synovial fluid, a substance that is like egg white and which lubricates the bone ends so that they slide over each other easily. Movable joints are also known as synovial joints, after the fluid.

Synovial fluid stops any friction (rubbing) between the bones that meet at the knee joint: the femur (thighbone), patella (kneecap), and tibia (shin).

33

Muscles

Muscle is the stretchy tissue that lets us move or keep still. We have around 650 skeletal muscles that pull the bones to which they are attached. The other types of muscle move our body organs. They are cardiac (heart) muscle and smooth muscle, which forms the walls of organs such as the stomach.

Fibrous Features

Skeletal muscle is made of long, strong fibers (strands) that can contract quickly and powerfully, but not for long. Cardiac muscle has short, crisscrossed fibers that keep moving rhythmically. The short fibers that make up smooth muscle form flat "sheets" that can contract for long periods.

The latissimus dorsi, or "lats," are the biggest muscles in the trunk (upper body). They stretch across the back from below the armpit.

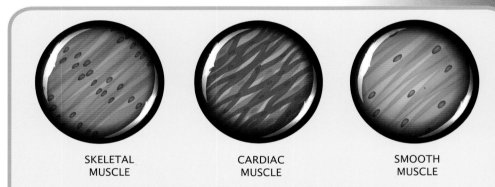

SKELETAL MUSCLE	CARDIAC MUSCLE	SMOOTH MUSCLE

Each muscle type has its own structure and its own job to do. Most of the muscle in the body is skeletal muscle.

BODY
BREAKTHROUGH

Scientist: Andreas Vesalius
Breakthrough: Described human muscles
Date: 1543
The story: Flemish anatomist Andreas Vesalius's *On the fabric of the human body* was a groundbreaking book on human anatomy. Vesalius dissected (cut up) dead bodies so he could study the muscles and other body systems at first hand. As a result, the illustrations in his book were incredibly detailed and accurate.

DID YOU KNOW? According to researchers at the University of Chicago, a frown uses 11 important facial muscles and a smile uses 12.

The deltoid is the triangular muscle at the top of the arm and shoulder. It connects to the collarbone, shoulder blade, and humerus.

The face has 43 muscles. They work together to pull the skin into thousands of different facial expressions.

The gluteus maximus, part of the buttocks, is the largest muscle in the body. Its job is to help keep us upright.

The pectoralis major (chest muscle) pulls the shoulder joint to make the upper arm move.

Muscle Structure

Skeletal muscle comes in many shapes, sizes, and strengths. The muscle tissue is made of bundles of muscle fibers that are called fascicles. Each fiber is composed of smaller strands called myofibrils. The myofibrils contain threads made out of different proteins.

FASCICLE (BUNDLE OF FIBERS)

BONE

MUSCLE FIBER

MYOFIBRIL

When nerve impulses from the brain make the myofibrils contract, the muscle fibers contract, too, and the fascicle pulls the bone to make it move.

SKELETAL MUSCLE TISSUE

Movement

Running, jumping, throwing … every single move we make depends on our muscles and how they act on our bones. Skeletal muscles are attached to bones by tendons. When they contract, they pull on the bone and make it move. Because muscles can only pull, not push, many of them work in pairs.

Opposing Pairs

Muscle pairs work together by performing opposite actions. When one muscle contracts, the other relaxes. The biceps and triceps muscles in the upper arm work together to let the arm bend or straighten.

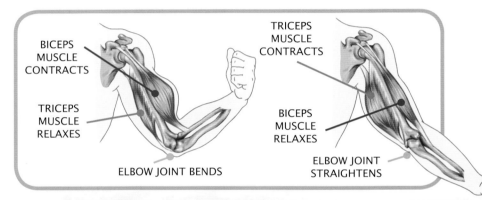

BICEPS MUSCLE CONTRACTS

TRICEPS MUSCLE RELAXES

ELBOW JOINT BENDS

TRICEPS MUSCLE CONTRACTS

BICEPS MUSCLE RELAXES

ELBOW JOINT STRAIGHTENS

Tendons and Ligaments

Strong cords of a protein called collagen attach bones and muscles. The ones that link bone to bone are called ligaments, and the ones that connect bone to muscle are tendons. Their fibers attach to the bone's outer membrane.

TENDON

CALF MUSCLES

HEEL BONE

The 15 cm/6 in-long Achilles tendon is the thickest, strongest tendon in the body. It stretches from the heel bone to the calf muscles.

When we jump, our Achilles tendons withstand loads up to ten times our body weight.

The triceps straightens the arm. Now the player can shoot the ball at the hoop with great force.

Nerve endings in the muscles contain sensors called proprioceptors. These gather information about the position of the body in space.

To work hard, muscles need lots of oxygen from the blood. If we're short of oxygen, we may get muscle cramps.

Muscles contain fast fibers that allow bursts of energy, and slow ones that help us keep going.

BODY BREAKTHROUGH

Scientists: Team at the Technical University of Munich (TUM)
Breakthrough: Microstructure of the Achilles tendon
Date: 2017
The story: Using a microscope that lit up different proteins, the team saw that where the Achilles tendon meets the heel bone, it splits into super-thin fibers. The cells of these fibers don't exactly match those of tendons—their proteins also share characteristics with cartilage, and this makes the bond especially strong.

DID YOU KNOW? In Greek myths, Achilles was a hero who died of an arrow wound in his heel. Today the phrase *Achilles heel* means "weak spot."

Skin

The skin is the body's largest organ. It helps to stop pathogens (harmful tiny organisms) entering the body. Its hairs and sweat glands keep our temperature steady. Its nerve endings let us touch.

Protective Layers

No more than 1.5 mm (0.06 in) thick even at its thickest places, the outer layer of skin (the epidermis) is kept waterproof by a fatty substance called sebum. It is where we shed old, dead skin cells—as many as 40,000 every minute! Just below the epidermis, the dermis has a rich blood supply, sense receptors, and glands. The final layer is the hypodermis, an insulating store of fat that lies directly over muscles, bones, and organs.

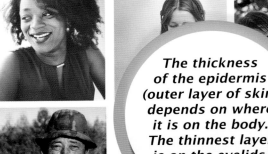

The thickness of the epidermis (outer layer of skin) depends on where it is on the body. The thinnest layer is on the eyelids.

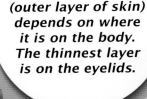

LAYERS OF THE SKIN

I EPIDERMIS
1. Pore
2. Surface layer of dead skin cells
3. Hair shaft

II DERMIS
4. Hair follicle
5. Coiled sweat gland
6. Sebum gland
7. Hair-raising muscle
8. Sensory nerve

III HYPODERMIS
9. Blood vessel
10. Fat

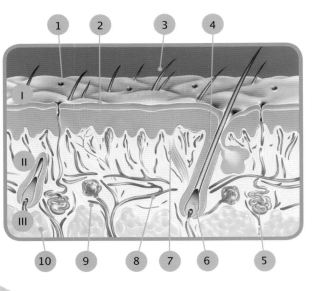

BODY
BREAKTHROUGH

Scientists: William Herschel and Henry Faulds
Breakthrough: Fingerprinting
Date: 1858 and 1880
The story: William Herschel, a civil servant in India (and grandson of the famous astronomer), used fingerprints to identify people on legal documents from 1858. However, Scottish physician Henry Faulds was the first to use them to solve a crime. In 1880 Faulds created a system for organizing types of fingerprint into groups.

DID YOU KNOW? Ridges on the skin of the fingertips form patterns that are unique to each person. Even identical twins have different fingerprints.

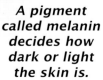

Marvelous Melanin

Melanin is a pigment found in the epidermis. It protects skin cells from the harmful effects of UV radiation, which is found in sunlight. It also darkens our skin and hair. People with darker skin are less likely to develop skin cancer.

Freckles are groups of skin cells that overproduce melanin. They are most visible on fair skin.

A pigment called melanin decides how dark or light the skin is.

Young skin is smooth and tight. Over time the epidermis will lose its elasticity.

Hair and Nails

How we do or don't style our hair—or even decorate our nails—determines our appearance and becomes part of our identity. But these body parts are not only about how we look. Made of a tough protein called keratin, they help to protect the body and do other important jobs, too.

Keratin Strands

Hairs are strands of tough, dead cells that push up from hair follicles (see page 40). Living cells at the base of the hair shaft divide to make the hair grow longer. Longer hairs protect the scalp and keep it warm. Shorter, finer hairs on the rest of the body make our skin sensitive to touch.

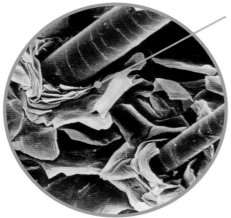

In this SEM scan, scalp hairs are magnified 1,320 times. Each hair has a flower–like cuticle at its base. Made of overlapping dead cells, the cuticle protects and strengthens the rest of the hair shaft.

Women from the Himba tribe of northwest Namibia are known for their elaborate hairstyles.

Himba hairstyles show a person's life stage. This style is for girls going through puberty.

BODY BREAKTHROUGH

Pioneers: Ancient Egyptians
Breakthrough: Use of henna as hair dye
Date: 1574 BCE
The story: Henna is a reddish–brown pigment made from the crushed, dried leaves of the henna plant. Indian body artists have used it to decorate the skin for more than 5,000 years. The first evidence of it as hair dye comes from the Egyptians. The mummy of Queen Ahmose-Henuttamehu (1574 BCE) has hennaed hair.

DID YOU KNOW? Xie Qiuping of China has the record for the longest head hair. When her hair was measured in 2004, it was 5.6 m (18.5 ft) long.

Nailing It

Like all primates, humans have fingernails instead of claws. We use them for many tasks, from scratching an itch to peeling fruit. Doctors can even tell how healthy we are by looking at them! Like hairs, nails develop from a living base, but the part we see is made of dead cells. Nails grow at a rate of around 1 mm (0.04 in) a week.

In 2015 Shridhar Chillal's left thumbnail was around 2 m (6.5 ft) long! The combined length of the nails on his left hand was about 9 m (30 ft).

The braids have been reddened with a mix of goat hair, butter, and ocher (a pigment from ground red rock).

41

Studying the Body

Without anatomy—the science of studying the body—we'd have no clue what the parts of the body do, or how to treat them if they go wrong. The first anatomy "book" was a papyrus written in Egypt in 1600 BCE, but our curiosity about the body's makeup dates back to prehistoric times.

Ways of Seeing

From the 1600s, anatomists no longer relied on just the naked eye—they had microscopes for a magnified view. Inner organs could only be seen after death, however, when a body could be cut open. X-rays, CT, MRI, and PET scans have made it possible to look inside living bodies.

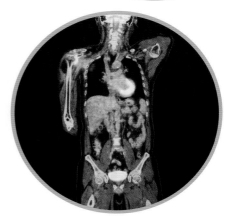

Anatomical drawing can reveal surprising details. These tendons move the fingers, which do not contain any muscles.

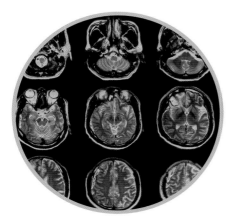

A magnetic resonance imaging (MRI) scanner builds up a picture from how atoms absorb and emit radio waves when they are in a magnetic field.

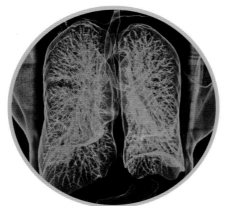

A computed tomography (CT) scan fires X-rays through the body from many angles and then joins together the resulting images to make a 2D or 3D image.

In positron emission tomography (PET), a radioactive chemical called a radiotracer is injected into the bloodstream. Scanning for the tracer gives detailed images of organs, tissue, and even electrical activity.

BODY BREAKTHROUGH

Scientist: Aristotle
Breakthrough: Comparative anatomy
Date: *c.* 350 BCE
The story: Greek philosopher Aristotle studied and compared the bodies of different animals. He believed that their similarities and differences would show him how all bodies worked, including the human body. The approach gave Aristotle lucky insights, but also made him draw some wrong conclusions about the body.

DID YOU KNOW? The 16th-century Flemist anatomist Andreas Vesalius used to dissect the corpses and body parts of hanged criminals.

Anatomy tells us that there are 27 bones in a human hand. In fact, more than half the bones in the body are found in the hands and feet.

"Scalpel, Please!"

Dissection—cutting up a body to explore its inner workings—has been taboo in almost all cultures at some time. It is still an essential part of a doctor's training, but some university hospitals now teach it using virtual reality (VR) technology.

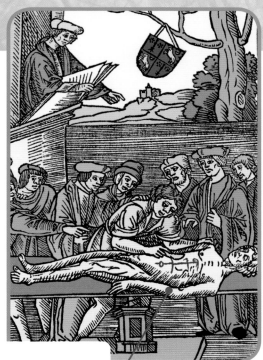

Italian anatomist Mondino de Luizza performs a dissection at the University of Bologna in 1315, just after the Church had lifted a ban on it.

Our word "anatomy" is taken from the Ancient Greek term "ἀνατομία," meaning "cutting up"—which is to say, dissection.

Spare Parts

From false teeth and wooden legs to lifelike robotic arms, we've used spare body parts, or prostheses, for thousands of years. If accident or disease stops an organ or limb functioning, a prosthesis can usually do the job. And, thanks to modern materials and technology, it can be hard to tell from the real thing!

Mechanical Stand-Ins

A pacemaker is a device that is fitted inside the chest. It produces electrical pulses that make the heart beat steadily. It is a kind of mechanical spare part, designed and made to copy a body function. Dialysis machines and ventilators are used to replace the kidneys and lungs.

This biobank stores human stem cells. In the future, they may be used to grow lifesaving new organs.

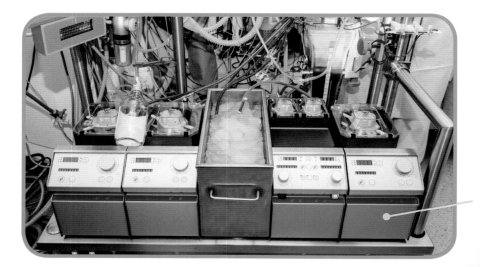

These blood stem cells will be used as living transplants. Their recipient will grow new blood cells.

This heart-lung machine is a temporary stand-in. It is used during surgery to take over from the patient's heart and lungs.

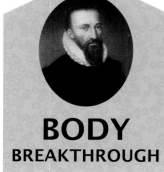

BODY
BREAKTHROUGH

Scientist: Ambroise Paré
Breakthrough: Prosthetic limbs that could move
Date: *c.* 1550
The story: French army surgeon Ambroise Paré noticed that soldiers who had a limb amputated (surgically removed) often became suicidal. He designed functional replacement limbs—his false legs bent at the knee and his arms at the elbow. Paré even invented a mechanical hand with jointed fingers that could grip.

Living Transplants

Organs or tissues donated by someone else are known as biological prostheses. Patients take powerful drugs to stop their immune system fighting the transplant. In the future, scientists hope to "grow" organs from patients' own tissues, so they won't be attacked.

This lab technician is isolating blood stem cells and tissue stem cells from an umbilical cord.

Surgeons around the world perform around 5,000 heart transplant operations every year.

DID YOU KNOW? In 2017 scientists from Manchester University, UK, grew the first working "mini–kidney" from human stem cells.

Heart and Lungs

Every minute that we're alive, our body is working to its own rhythms: the beat of our heart, and the rise and fall of our lungs. These two vital organs work together. They deliver the oxygen that we need for life and take away waste carbon dioxide.

The Basics

When we breathe, we draw oxygen down into our lungs. Blood flowing through the lungs transports the oxygen around the body. The blood keeps moving because of the actions of our very own pump: the heart.

Seen from below in a CT scan, this heart has been partly dissected to show the left atrium and ventricle. On either side are the branching blood vessels (red) and air passages (blue) in the lungs.

LEFT ATRIUM

LEFT VENTRICLE

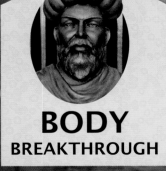

BODY
BREAKTHROUGH

Scientist: Ibn al–Nafis
Breakthrough: Described the pulmonary circulation of the blood
Date: 1242
The story: Syrian doctor and anatomist Ibn al–Nafis was the first to describe the way that blood vessels carry blood from the right side of the heart to the lungs to pick up oxygen and then return that blood to the left side of the heart. From there, it travels around the body, releasing the oxygen where needed, before returning to the heart.

Where this Sherpa lives, at high altitudes, there is a very low concentration of oxygen in the air.

Sherpas are Nepalese mountain guides. After living in the Himalayas for centuries, they've evolved to cope with less oxygen.

Oxygen Cycle

The lungs and airways form the respiratory system, while our heart and blood vessels make up the cardiovascular system. Oxygen and carbon dioxide enter and leave our lungs through small blood vessels called capillaries by gas exchange—the swapping of one gas for another. They are carried around the body via the cardiovascular system.

OXYGEN (O_2)

CARBON DIOXIDE (CO_2)

LUNGS

RED BLOOD CELLS

ORGANS

Sherpas' cells are different to most people's. Their mitochondria produce more energy from less oxygen.

Sherpas have thinner blood that flows easily at high altitude. They also have more capillaries and can carry oxygen more efficiently to muscles, tissues, and organs.

Even at rest, our blood must pass through the lungs about 15 times a minute to provide our organs with enough oxygen.

DID YOU KNOW? The thin atmosphere on top of Everest means that every breath contains one-third less oxygen than at sea level.

Breathing

Breathing's essential to life, but we can also have fun with it. To blow bubbles, we take a deeper breath and control how we exhale it.

During a day we take more than 20,000 breaths—but most of the time, we don't even notice! Our lungs inflate and deflate automatically, controlled by the brain, which alters how deeply we breathe, and how fast, in response to what we're doing.

Journey to the Lungs

From the mouth or nostril, air passes through the throat (pharynx). A flap called the epiglottis stops food or drink entering the windpipe (trachea). As it reaches the lungs, the windpipe branches into two airways called the main bronchi.

A bubble is a mixture of water and soap that's been filled with air we've breathed out.

The trachea is the largest airway in the respiratory system. In most adults it is about 11 cm (4.3 in) long and 2 cm (0.8 in) across.

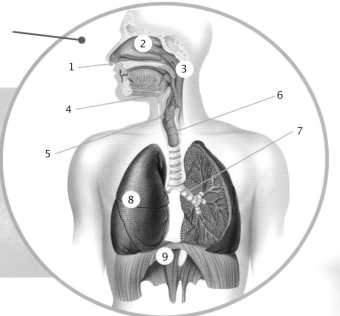

RESPIRATORY SYSTEM

1. Nostril
2. Nasal cavity
3. Pharynx (throat)
4. Epiglottis
5. Larynx (voicebox)
6. Trachea (windpipe)
7. Bronchus
8. Lung
9. Diaphragm

We can breathe through the nose or mouth. Nasal breathing allows the lungs to take in more oxygen, and the nasal cavity filters and warms the air.

BODY BREAKTHROUGH

Scientists: Wei Zuo and team, Tongji University, China
Breakthrough: First lung stem cell transplant
Date: 2018
The story: In 2015 Professor Wei Zuo's team found stem cells in mice that regrew damaged bronchioles (see page 50) and other lung structures. Since then, he has found stem cells to do this in humans. Zuo has transplanted patients' own lung stem cells to a damaged part of their lung and seen it recover.

DID YOU KNOW? Every minute, about 5,500 cm² (9.5 pt) of air pass into and out of the lungs.

Not blowing enough won't form a bubble. Blowing too hard will make the bubble pop.

Pouting the lips creates a narrower stream of air. We can blow faster and more accurately.

In and Out

The diaphragm is a sheet of muscle between the lungs and abdomen. When we inhale (breathe in), the diaphragm flattens and makes room for the lungs to inflate. When we exhale (breathe out), the diaphragm relaxes again.

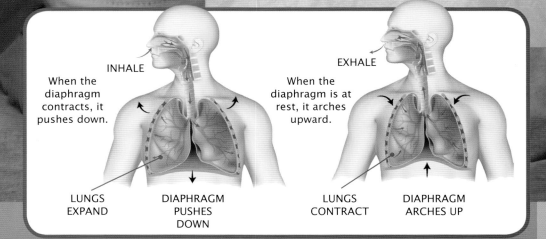

INHALE

When the diaphragm contracts, it pushes down.

EXHALE

When the diaphragm is at rest, it arches upward.

LUNGS EXPAND   DIAPHRAGM PUSHES DOWN

LUNGS CONTRACT   DIAPHRAGM ARCHES UP

Inside the Lungs

We inflate and deflate our lungs as we breathe, but that doesn't mean they're balloon-like bags that fill with air and then empty. The lungs feel like soft sponges, because of the hundreds of millions of tiny airways inside them. This structure also means that the lungs are easy to damage.

The left lung is smaller than the right because of the space taken up by the heart.

Branching Out

Inside the lungs, the two main bronchi split into smaller and smaller branches called bronchioles. Each bronchiole ends in a tiny air sac called an alveolus.

Alveoli look like miniature bunches of grapes. Each one is covered in a mesh of tiny blood vessels that take away oxygen in exchange for carbon dioxide.

Having a Clearout

Coughing or sneezing clears our airways and forces out dust, pollen, mucus, or other irritating particles. Viral infections, such as the common cold, can cause coughs and sneezes. Lung damage from smoking can also cause a dry cough and shortness of breath.

A single sneeze can produce 40,000 droplets of germ–laden mucus, most too tiny to see with the naked eye.

This CT scan shows a normal, healthy heart and lungs, seen from below.

BODY BREAKTHROUGH

Scientist: John Mudge
Breakthrough: Invented the inhaler
Date: 1778
The story: English doctor John Mudge invented the Mudge Inhaler to treat people with coughs. It was a tankard with a lid and flexible breathing tube. Hot water was poured in, along with herbs or a painkiller such as opium or ether, and the patient breathed it all in as steam through the tube.

VERTEBRA   ESOPHAGUS

Around 700 million alveoli in the lungs create a huge surface area where gas exchange can take place.

LEFT LUNG

RIGHT LUNG

HEART

The lung is spongy, made up of branching networks of air passages and blood vessels.

DID YOU KNOW? The alveoli in the lungs have a combined surface area of around 70 m² (753 sq ft)—the same as five parking spaces.

Blood Vessels

The main types of blood vessel are arteries, veins, and capillaries. Arteries carry blood *away from* the heart, and veins transport blood *to* it. Capillaries, the smallest blood vessels, connect the arteries and veins. Their thin walls allow oxygen and nutrients *out* into nearby cells, and take any waste *in*.

Arteries and Veins

Arteries have thick, muscular walls that contract to help pump the blood. Veins transport blood at lower pressures, so they have thinner walls. One-way valves in the veins make sure that the "used" blood flows toward the heart.

CAPILLARIES

VALVE

MUSCLE LINING

ARTERY

VEIN

Capillary Beds

Oxygen, nutrients, and waste are exchanged in the capillary beds—the meshes of capillaries that crisscross the body's tissues and organs. Capillary walls are just one cell thick, so gases and other substances easily pass through them.

This SEM scan shows red blood cells in a capillary in the liver. They are bringing nutrients from the intestines and oxygen from the heart.

BODY
BREAKTHROUGH

Scientist: Moses Maimonides
Breakthrough: Described arteries, veins, and capillaries
Date: 1190s
The story: In *The Medical Aphorisms of Moses*, the 12th–century Jewish physician Moses Maimonides explained the difference between "pulsating" arteries and "non–pulsating" veins. He also described narrow vessels, too small to see, which connected arteries and veins, and allowed an exchange of blood and gases.

This is the aorta, the largest artery and the main artery out of the heart.

In this artwork, oxygen-rich arteries are shown in red. Oxygen-poor veins blood are blue.

The superior vena cava carries blood from the upper body back to the heart.

The heart is a hollow pump, about the size of a fist. It's protected by the ribcage.

This vein, the inferior vena cava, carries blood from the lower body back to the heart.

This artery, the descending aorta, takes oxygenated blood to the chest, ribs, and lower half of the body.

DID YOU KNOW? Placed in a line, an adult's blood vessels would measure 160,935 km (100,000 miles)—enough to circle the Earth four times.

Circulation

We need good circulation for our body to function. The force that makes our blood circulate (move around the body) is called our blood pressure. If it's too low, not enough oxygen and nutrients reach the organs. If it's too high, it puts stress on the organs, especially the heart.

Exercise strengthens the heart, makes the cardiovascular system healthier, and improves our circulation.

Double Circuit

Blood circulates the body in two circuits. One circuit is called the pulmonary circulation. It takes blood to the lungs to be oxygenated. The second circuit is called the systemic circulation, and it transports oxygen-rich blood to every part of the body.

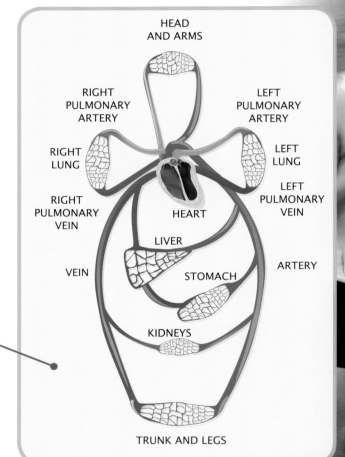

HEAD AND ARMS

RIGHT PULMONARY ARTERY

LEFT PULMONARY ARTERY

RIGHT LUNG

LEFT LUNG

RIGHT PULMONARY VEIN

LEFT PULMONARY VEIN

HEART

LIVER

VEIN

STOMACH

ARTERY

KIDNEYS

TRUNK AND LEGS

This diagram shows the pulmonary circulation in blue and the systemic circulation in red.

BODY BREAKTHROUGH

Scientist: Scipione Riva-Rocci
Breakthrough: Invented the cuff-based blood pressure monitor
Date: 1896
The story: Austrian doctor Samuel von Basch invented the first sphygmomanometer (*sfig-moh-ma-NOH-mee-tuh*) in 1881, but it was fragile and awkward to use. Fifteen years later, Italian doctor Scipione Riva-Rocci came up with a much handier version that had an inflatable cuff for the arm—a simple design that is still used today.

DID YOU KNOW? During its 120-day lifespan, a red blood cell travels about 485 km (300 miles) around the body.

Taking the Pressure

Blood pressure is a measure of the force that your heart uses to pump blood around the body (see pages 58–59). Pressure is highest as the heart pumps blood out (systolic pressure) and lowest while the heart fills with blood (diastolic pressure).

Ideally, systolic blood pressure is 90–120 mmHg (millimeters of mercury), and diastolic pressure 60–80 mmHg.

Taking someone's pulse—counting the rhythmic "waves" at the wrist—tells us their heart rate.

During a marathon, the average runner's heart rate is 160 beats per minute.

A marathon runner's blood pressure is lower than average. At rest, their systolic pressure is around 105 mmHg and their diastolic 65 mmHg. We say this as "105/65."

The Heart

PARTS OF THE HEART
1. Superior vena cava
2. Inferior vena cava
3. Right atrium
4. Right ventricle
5. Pulmonary artery
6. Pulmonary veins
7. Left atrium
8. Left ventricle
9. Aorta (main artery)

Over an average lifetime, the heart beats more than three billion times. This hollow, muscular organ never stops. Every minute it pumps about 5 liters (1 gallon) of blood through the lungs and around the body.

Blood Flow

The heart has four chambers, in two linked pairs—a pair of atria and a pair of ventricles. The right atrium and right ventricle receive oxygen-poor blood and pass it on to the lungs. The left atrium and ventricle receive oxygen-rich blood from the lungs and pass it on to the body.

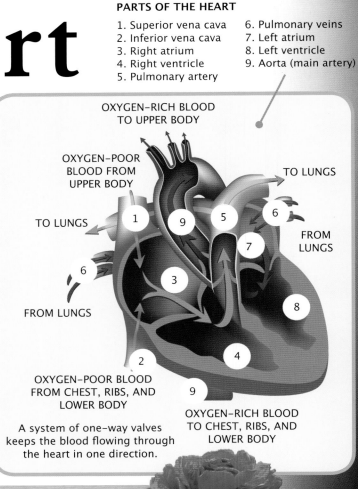

OXYGEN-RICH BLOOD TO UPPER BODY

OXYGEN-POOR BLOOD FROM UPPER BODY

TO LUNGS

TO LUNGS

FROM LUNGS

FROM LUNGS

OXYGEN-POOR BLOOD FROM CHEST, RIBS, AND LOWER BODY

OXYGEN-RICH BLOOD TO CHEST, RIBS, AND LOWER BODY

A system of one-way valves keeps the blood flowing through the heart in one direction.

Seat of the Soul

The heart has been a powerful symbol in many cultures, used to represent affection and love. It can be stylized (❤) or look like an anatomical heart. In Mexico, Roman Catholics wear the heart as a symbol of Jesus's love for humankind.

At a parade for the Mexican Day of the Dead (31 October), this woman's fancy dress includes a "heart" with dummy blood vessels.

BODY
BREAKTHROUGH

Scientist: Nina Starr Braunwald
Breakthrough: Implanted the first artificial heart valve
Date: 1960
The story: The USA's first female cardiac surgeon, Nina Starr Braunwald, used a prosthetic heart valve that she'd designed to perform the first successful valve replacement. She also designed the Braunwald-Cutter valve (left), which was the first to have cloth-covered struts to make patients less uncomfortable.

DID YOU KNOW? The ancient Egyptians tucked amulets shaped like real hearts into mummies' bandages to protect the dead.

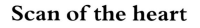

Scan of the heart

Inside the heart, a wall of muscle called the septum separates the right atrium and ventricle from the left.

SUPERIOR VENA CAVA

AORTA

The heart has its own network of blood vessels—the coronary system—to supply blood to the heart muscle.

LEFT ATRIUM

RIGHT ATRIUM

GREAT CARDIAC VEIN

LEFT VENTRICLE

RIGHT VENTRICLE

Coronary arteries bring oxygen-rich blood to the heart and coronary veins take oxygen-poor blood away.

Ventricles have thicker, more muscular walls than atria. They have to pump the blood farther and with more force.

The Heart Cycle

At rest, an adult's heart beats 60 to 100 times a minute. Each cycle has a pause or rest, followed by a "duh-dum." The "duh" is valves closing as blood leaves the atria; the "dum" is valves closing as blood leaves the ventricles.

One Direction

One-way valves control the flow of blood through the heart, so that it enters the atria and the ventricles at alternate times. The heart muscle squeezes tight (contracts) and then relaxes, which opens and shuts the valves.

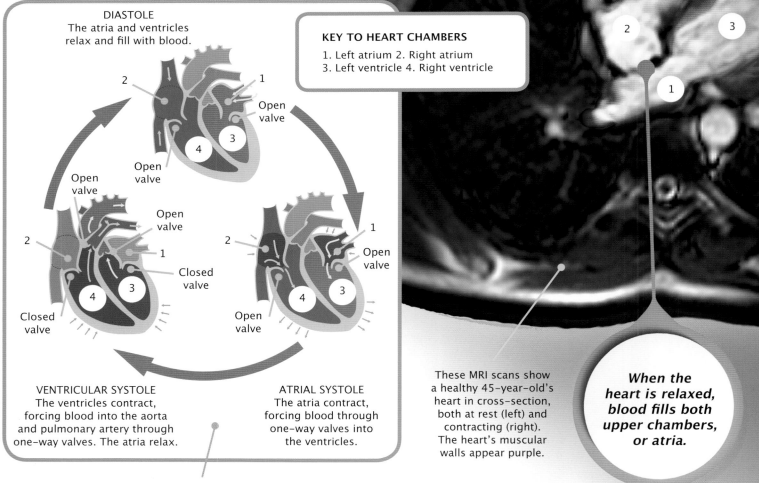

DIASTOLE
The atria and ventricles relax and fill with blood.

1
2
Open valve
Open valve
3
4
Open valve

KEY TO HEART CHAMBERS
1. Left atrium 2. Right atrium
3. Left ventricle 4. Right ventricle

Open valve
1
2
Closed valve
3
4
Closed valve

Open valve
1
2
3
4
Open valve

VENTRICULAR SYSTOLE
The ventricles contract, forcing blood into the aorta and pulmonary artery through one-way valves. The atria relax.

ATRIAL SYSTOLE
The atria contract, forcing blood through one-way valves into the ventricles.

The heart's pumping mechanism follows a constant cycle of rest (diastole) and contraction (systole).

These MRI scans show a healthy 45-year-old's heart in cross-section, both at rest (left) and contracting (right). The heart's muscular walls appear purple.

When the heart is relaxed, blood fills both upper chambers, or atria.

Steady Beat

Most of us have a regular heartbeat—the chambers of the heart contract and relax at a steady rate. The contractions are triggered by regular electrical pulses, sent from special cells in the walls of the right atrium.

RELAXATION (DIASTOLE)

CONTRACTION (SYSTOLE)

An artificial pacemaker can save the life of a patient with an irregular heartbeat. It sends out electrical pulses to make the heart beat.

This scan shows the lower chambers, or ventricles, squeezing out blood—the process of ventricular systole.

4

2

3

1

The blood pumps out of the left ventricle through this artery called the aorta.

Scientist: William Harvey
Breakthrough: Explained how the heart worked
Date: 1616
The story: Personal doctor to two English kings, William Harvey was the first scientist to accurately describe the function of the heart and one-way circulation of the blood, and be able to back up his theory with evidence. He presented his ideas to the Royal College of Physicians in 1616, and published them 12 years later.

BODY
BREAKTHROUGH

DID YOU KNOW? The implantable pacemaker was invented by an American, Wilson Greatbatch. It was first fitted in 1960.

The Blood

Blood—the remarkable red liquid that flows through our arteries and veins—is made up of three types of blood cell floating in a yellowy fluid called plasma. As well as transporting oxygen, waste, and nutrients, blood helps us fight off infection and is an important part of our immune system.

Blood Cell Types

Most of our blood cells are the red ones that give blood its hue. They make up around 50 percent of the blood's volume in men, and 40 percent in women. The other types are white blood cells (see pages 62–63) and platelets.

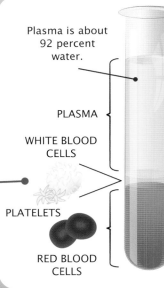

Plasma is about 92 percent water.

PLASMA

WHITE BLOOD CELLS

PLATELETS

RED BLOOD CELLS

Around 55 percent of the blood is plasma. Many useful substances are dissolved in plasma, including proteins, electrolytes, sugars, hormones, and vitamins.

Blood Clots

Platelets are shapeshifters. Usually plate-shaped, they turn spiky if a blood vessel is damaged. This shape helps the platelets to cling together and form a clot to plug the damage. Clots are a healthy response to injury—they help us heal.

These red blood cells have formed a clot called a thrombus. It can be dangerous if it blocks the flow of blood.

BODY
BREAKTHROUGH

Scientist: Jan Swammerdam
Breakthrough: First to see red blood cells
Date: 1658
The story: Dutch biologist Jan Swammerdam was the first to describe red blood cells—he had studied the blood of a frog through an early microscope. Sixteen years later another Dutch scientist, Antoine van Leeuwenhoek, made his own observations of red blood cells. He named them "corpuscles."

DID YOU KNOW? In a typical day, an adult makes 200 billion new red blood cells, 10 billion white ones, and 400 billion platelets.

This is a B-lymphocyte, a kind of white blood cell. It is covered with microscopic, hairlike projections called microvilli.

This artwork shows blood cells pouring from a cut vein.

Platelet

In blood stored for transfusion, some red blood cells lose water and shrink into spiky "burr" cells. Minutes after entering the body, the plasma will help them regain water and their normal shape.

Leukocyte (white blood cell)

Red blood cells contain an iron-rich protein and pigment called hemoglobin.

Red blood cells function for about four months, then die. Their iron is reused in future red blood cells.

Soldier Cells

1. The surface of the pathogens is covered with protein molecules called antigens.

White blood cells, or leukocytes, make up only one percent of our blood, but they are very important. They help to defend our body against infection by tracking down and destroying invaders such as bacteria and viruses. Along with the lymphatic system, they make up part of the immune system.

White Blood Cells in Action

Some white blood cells surround and digest pathogens (invaders that cause disease). Others release killer chemicals—antibodies, which destroy pathogens, or antitoxins, which neutralize their harmful effects.

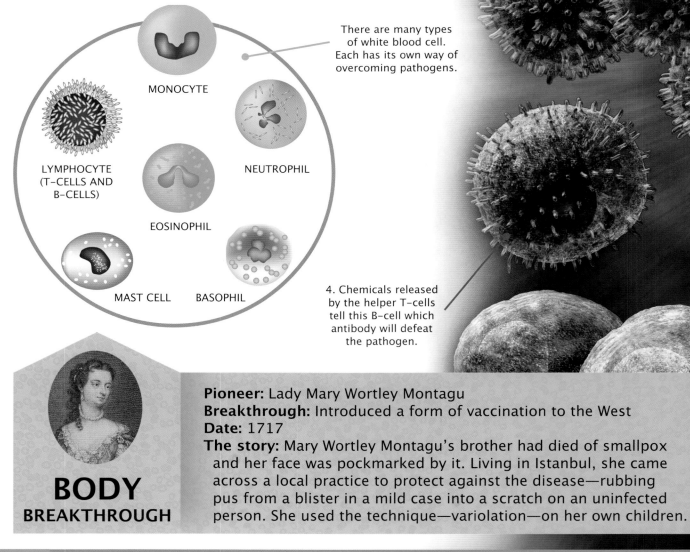

There are many types of white blood cell. Each has its own way of overcoming pathogens.

MONOCYTE

LYMPHOCYTE (T–CELLS AND B–CELLS)

NEUTROPHIL

EOSINOPHIL

MAST CELL

BASOPHIL

4. Chemicals released by the helper T–cells tell this B–cell which antibody will defeat the pathogen.

BODY BREAKTHROUGH

Pioneer: Lady Mary Wortley Montagu
Breakthrough: Introduced a form of vaccination to the West
Date: 1717
The story: Mary Wortley Montagu's brother had died of smallpox and her face was pockmarked by it. Living in Istanbul, she came across a local practice to protect against the disease—rubbing pus from a blister in a mild case into a scratch on an uninfected person. She used the technique—variolation—on her own children.

DID YOU KNOW? Allergic reactions happen when white blood cells attack harmless "invaders" with histamine, which causes rashes or swelling.

Filtering Fluid

The lymphatic system transports lymph—a fluid containing infection-fighting white blood cells—throughout the body. The lymph is filtered through bean-shaped lymph nodes. We have hundreds of nodes packed with lymphocytes. Nodes can swell up when fighting an infection.

2. This macrophage has engulfed the pathogen. It now has small amounts of antigen on its surface. This tells other white blood cells how to fight the pathogen.

3. There are two types of T-cell: helpers and killers. This helper T-cell recognizes the antigen. It activates an army of B-cells to destroy it.

5. This plasma cell formed from a B-cell. It makes one type of antibody—a match for the antigen.

6. The antibodies weaken the pathogen by locking on to its antigens. They also attract more macrophages that will engulf it.

LYMPHATIC SYSTEM

1. Tonsils contain T-cells and B-cells.
2. Thymus gland is where T-cells mature.
3. Armpit nodes filter lymph from the arms and breast, and drain it from the chest wall.
4. Spleen stores monocytes that can turn into dendritic cells or macrophages.
5. Thoracic duct is the largest lymph vessel.
6. Cisterna chyli receives lymph from the lower body.
7. Groin nodes filter lymph from the lower body.

Blood Medicine

Blood is no good at keeping secrets—it gives doctors all sorts of clues about patient health. Testing for sugars, proteins, and other substances reveals how well the heart, liver, or other organs are working. Certain diseases show up in the blood, too, such as cancers, anemia, diabetes, and heart disease.

Blood Types

Our immune system doesn't attack its own red blood cells because it recognizes the antigens on their surface. Within any blood group (A, B, AB, or O), the markers match. Red blood cells from a different blood group have different protein markers and usually trigger an immune response.

Today, diabetics can self-test to check glucose levels in their blood. If there's too much, they will need an injection of insulin.

Putting blood from one person (the donor) into another is called a transfusion. It saves lives, but can also be fatal if the donor's blood group doesn't match the recipient's. The exception is blood group O, which is compatible with all the other groups.

Before 1916, when blood storage became a reality, transfusions were direct. In this 1882 engraving, blood from the donor goes straight into the patient.

The Need for Blood

Blood transfusions help patients who lose a lot of blood after surgery or an injury. Human patients first received donor blood in 1667—but from sheep, not other people! By the 1800s, doctors were performing human-to-human transfusions. However, they didn't know about blood groups, so patients often reacted badly.

Fingerstick devices can collect a droplet of blood for testing. They contain a sharp, sterile needle that pierces the skin.

The resulting drop of blood will be put on a test strip. A portable meter will measure its glucose levels.

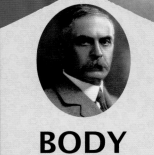

BODY
BREAKTHROUGH

Scientist: Karl Landsteiner
Breakthrough: Classified the major blood groups
Date: 1901-2
The story: Austrian biologist Karl Landsteiner identified blood groups A, B, and O (which he called C) in 1901, and AB in 1902. He realized blood transfusions must be from matching groups—otherwise, the patient's antibodies would fight the "alien" blood and their red blood cells would clump together in dangerous clots.

DID YOU KNOW? Eighty-five percent of us have RhD positive blood (our red blood cells have the antigen RhD). The rest of us are RhD negative.

Food for Energy

Everything we do uses energy: breathing or keeping warm; running a race or washing the dishes; reading a book or planning a trip. The body also needs energy so that it can grow, repair itself, and fight off disease.

Food Processor

Carbohydrates are our main source of energy. Our digestive system breaks them down into glucose, a natural sugar. Carbohydrates are found in foods such as bread, rice, pasta, potatoes, vegetables, and fruit.

Breakdancing takes strength, timing, and energy. The toughest moves are freezes, where the body stops and holds a balance.

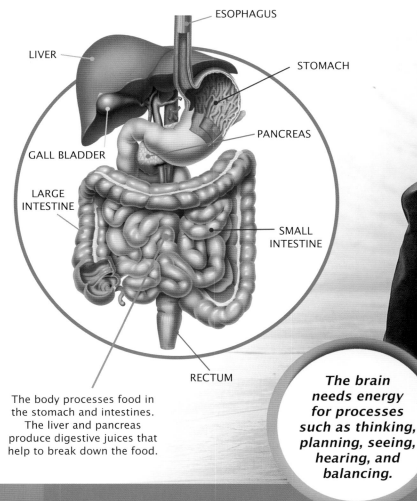

ESOPHAGUS

LIVER

STOMACH

PANCREAS

GALL BLADDER

LARGE INTESTINE

SMALL INTESTINE

RECTUM

The body processes food in the stomach and intestines. The liver and pancreas produce digestive juices that help to break down the food.

The brain needs energy for processes such as thinking, planning, seeing, hearing, and balancing.

Muscles convert glucose from the bloodstream into energy for motion and heat.

Fuel Reserves

Food contains fats. We store fats in adipocytes (fat cells) in a form that can be released if our body needs energy and has little or no glucose. Fat cells also help us to stay warm and cushion us from bumps and bruises.

This SEM scan shows the individual fat cells that make up fatty tissue. The capillaries (blue) that transport fats to and from the cell are also visible.

People who use up the energy from food quickly are said to have a fast metabolism. People who don't are said to have a slow metabolism.

BODY BREAKTHROUGH

Scientist: Andreas Marggraf
Breakthrough: Isolated glucose
Date: 1747
The story: German chemist Andreas Marggraf isolated glucose from raisins in 1747. He also found a way to extract sugar from beets. Tropical sugarcane had been the only source of sugar until then. Marggraf's discovery meant Europeans could grow their own sugar crop.

DID YOU KNOW? According to the World Health Organization, in 2016 two-fifths of adults were overweight (had an unhealthy amount of fat cells).

A Balanced Diet

As well as being a source of glucose and fat, food provides other vital substances including proteins, vitamins, minerals, and fiber. Eating a range of different foods helps our body to function and stay healthy.

Starchy carbohydrates, such as rice, provide energy, contain fiber, and help the body to feel full for longer.

Perfect Plate

A balanced diet is mostly fruit, vegetables, and carbohydrates, with lesser amounts of protein and dairy. It does not include foods high in saturated fat, salt, or sugar. These unhealthy foods can be occasional treats, but it's good to remember there are many delicious foods that are good for us.

STARCHY CARBOHYDRATES

FRUIT AND VEGETABLES

DAIRY

FATS AND SUGARS

PROTEINS

Vitamins and Minerals

Foods also contain "micronutrients" that do important jobs. Vitamins include A, which helps our vision, and C, which fights disease and makes collagen (the main protein in skin and connective tissue). Minerals include iron, which transports oxygen around the body, and calcium, which is essential for healthy bones and teeth.

This food wheel shows how much of our diet should be made up by each food group.

Most people don't need supplements—we can get all our vitamins and minerals from a healthy diet.

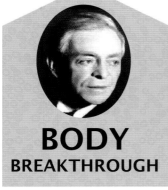

BODY BREAKTHROUGH

Scientist: Casimir Funk
Breakthrough: Discovered vitamins
Date: 1912
The story: Polish biochemist Casimir Funk discovered vitamin B_3, the substance in brown rice that prevents the disease beriberi. He predicted the existence of more protective nutrients (vitamins B_1, B_2, C, and D). Funk thought they'd all be amines (nitrogen–based compounds) like B_3, so he called them "vitamines" (vital amines).

DID YOU KNOW? Long before the discovery of vitamin C, 16th-century sailors noticed that eating oranges, lemons, and limes prevented the disease scurvy.

Fruit and vegetables provide vitamins, minerals, plant chemicals, and fiber.

In some cultures, people eat very little dairy. They prefer to eat leafy vegetables for calcium, and other foods for proteins and fats.

Seafood is a source of protein. We need protein to build and repair the cells that make up our muscles, cartilage, bones, skin, and blood.

The Digestive Process

The aroma of delicious food can start off the digestive process before food has even passed our lips. Cooking smells make our mouth water—glands in our mouth produce saliva that will play a part in the first stage of breaking food down.

Physical and Chemical Digestion

On its twisty path through the digestive system, food breaks down in two ways. Being chewed in the mouth and churned in the stomach tears it into smaller pieces. This is a physical change. Then substances called enzymes set off chemical reactions that break food molecules into smaller molecules that can be absorbed by the blood.

When we see appealing food, our brain sends messages to the digestive system, preparing it for action.

Enzymes produced in the small intestine can turn starch into sugars, protein into amino acids, and fat into fatty acids and glycerol.

As we bring food to the mouth, we produce saliva. This will moisten the food so it is easy to swallow.

DID YOU KNOW? The time from food entering the mouth to its waste leaving the body as feces (poop) can sometimes be as long as 72 hours.

Scientist: William Beaumont
Breakthrough: Discovered chemical digestion
Date: 1820s
The story: In 1822 American doctor William Beaumont treated fur trader Alex St Martin for a shot in the stomach. He saved the man's life, but the fistula (hole) never fully healed. Beaumont employed St Martin and, over the next decade, used his open stomach to conduct experiments and study the stages of digestion. He published his findings in 1833.

Indigestion

Stress, overeating, gobbling food too fast, and eating junk food can all result in indigestion. Ulcers (open sores) in the stomach or small intestine can cause it, too. The symptoms include stomach pain, gas, and feeling bloated.

Indigestion can create an uncomfortable burning sensation.

Food can have meaning. These tangyuan (round rice dumplings) symbolize family togetherness.

As well as keeping us alive, food contributes to our mental well-being. Eating with family or friends keeps us connected.

Inside the Mouth

Digestion begins in the mouth. The front teeth (incisors and canines) cut the food, and the back ones (premolars and molars) chew it. Saliva—which contains mucus, antibodies, and enzymes, but is mostly water—prepares the chewed-up food for its journey.

Super Saliva

Mucus in the saliva makes the food slimy so that it will slide down the throat (esophagus). Antibodies help to kill off bacteria in food before they enter the body. Enzymes start to break down the food chemically.

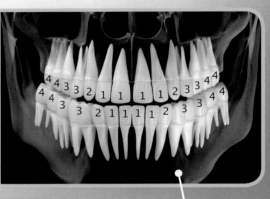

ADULT TEETH AND ROOTS
1. Incisors
2. Canines
3. Premolars
4. Molars

Adults have 32 teeth. This illustration doesn't include the wisdom teeth (third molars), which are the last teeth to come through.

How We Swallow

Our tongue shapes the chewed-up, moistened food into a ball (bolus) and pushes it to the back of the mouth. As the top of the gullet (esophagus) opens, the airways are briefly blocked by the epiglottis, tongue, and palate. This reflex action stops our breathing for a split second, and prevents us from choking.

When the bolus is at the back of the mouth (1), the airways automatically close (2). Once it's in the esophagus (3), they reopen.

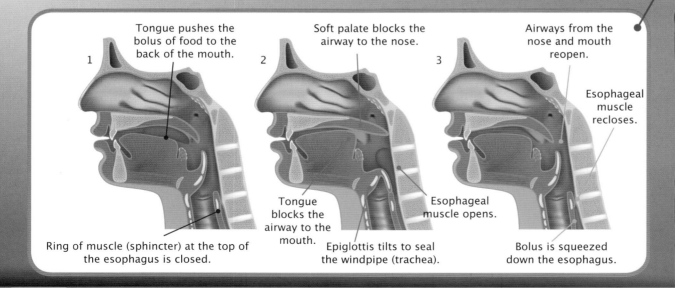

1
Tongue pushes the bolus of food to the back of the mouth.

Ring of muscle (sphincter) at the top of the esophagus is closed.

2
Soft palate blocks the airway to the nose.

Tongue blocks the airway to the mouth.

Epiglottis tilts to seal the windpipe (trachea).

Esophageal muscle opens.

3
Airways from the nose and mouth reopen.

Esophageal muscle recloses.

Bolus is squeezed down the esophagus.

> *Glands in the mouth release up to 4 liters (7 pints) of saliva a day. It is 99 percent water.*

Children have fewer teeth than adults—ten in the upper jaw, and ten in the bottom. Between the ages of 6 and 12, these teeth drop out and the adult teeth push through.

Plaque is a mixture of leftover food, saliva, and acid-releasing bacteria. If we don't brush our teeth, the plaque can damage tooth enamel and create cavities.

> *Enamel is the hard, white coating that protects teeth from acids in our saliva and produced by bacteria.*

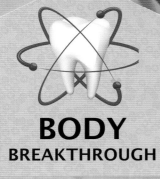

BODY BREAKTHROUGH

Scientist: Frederick McKay
Breakthrough: Discovered that the mineral fluoride protects teeth
Date: 1930
The story: In 1909 Colorado Springs dentist Frederick McKay noticed that his patients had awful-looking, mottled teeth—but no tooth decay! By 1930 he'd proved that something in the water supply was staining but also strengthening their teeth. Tests the following year showed that the water had high levels of fluoride.

DID YOU KNOW? The ancient Etruscans made false teeth as early as the 700s BCE, but the oldest known set of dentures is just 400–700 years old.

Mouth to Stomach

This illustration is based on a CT scan of the neck.

From the throat, the bolus is squeezed along the gullet (esophagus) in rhythmic, rippling waves, called peristalsis. It is pushed to the stomach, a stretchy bag that makes highly acidic gastric juices. Rings of muscle (sphincters) at the stomach's entrance and exit stop the juices escaping.

Inside the Stomach

The muscular walls of the stomach squash and churn the food. They mix it with gastric juices, which are packed with enzymes that start off chemical reactions. The mashed-up food turns into a partly digested, bitter "soup" called chyme.

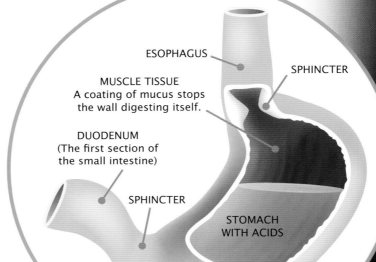

ESOPHAGUS

SPHINCTER

MUSCLE TISSUE
A coating of mucus stops the wall digesting itself.

DUODENUM
(The first section of the small intestine)

SPHINCTER

STOMACH WITH ACIDS

As well as digesting food, the stomach can store it until there's room in the intestines. In most adults it can hold around 1 l (1.8 pt).

BODY BREAKTHROUGH

Scientist: Henry Heimlich
Breakthrough: Invented the Heimlich maneuver
Date: 1974
The story: The traditional first aid response to choking was a slap on the back. US surgeon Henry Heimlich believed his maneuver was more likely to dislodge the object blocking the airway and make it shoot out. It involved standing behind the patient and applying strong abdominal thrusts—pushing hard on the bottom of the diaphragm.

DID YOU KNOW? The stomach secretes hydrochloric acid, a substance strong enough to dissolve a thin metal bar!

The pharynx (throat) connects the mouth and nose to the esophagus, trachea (windpipe), and layrynx (voicebox).

A sphincter at the top of the esophagus opens only to allow a bolus of food to pass through.

Adaptable Tube

The lining of the esophagus can stretch and expand thanks to its microscopic folds. They create a ridged surface that protects the esophagus from being scratched by food particles.

This SEM scan reveals the ridges on the esophagus's lining and some of its rod-shaped bacteria.

The muscular walls of the esophagus contract to push the food to the stomach, in a process called peristalsis.

Up to 25 cm (9.8 in) long in adults, the esophagus is the narrowest part of the digestive tract.

The Intestines

From the stomach, the chyme is pushed through the coiled tubes that make up the intestines. Its nutrients pass through their walls (see pages 78–79). Whatever's left forms feces (poop) and passes out of the anus.

Recipe for Poop

The small intestine absorbs about 90 percent of the water we take in. The large intestine absorbs most of the rest, leaving a little to keep feces soft. Feces are made of undigested food, digested substances that weren't absorbed, millions of bacteria, old cells from the gut lining, and undigestible salts.

Ridged folds in the middle section of a healthy duodenum make the chyme spiral and slow down. This allows time for the nutrients to be fully absorbed.

"Friendly" Bacteria

Living in our gut is a community of tens of trillions of microbes, including up to 1,000 species of bacteria. Some are probiotics, or "friendly" bacteria, that help to break down our food and also fight the pathogens (germs) that cause sickness and diarrhea.

Fermented foods such as sauerkraut contain probiotics that improve our gut health.

BODY BREAKTHROUGH

Scientists: Hippocrates and his followers
Breakthrough: Described parasitic intestinal worms (left)
Date: c. 500s BCE
The story: The *Hippocratic Corpus*, a set of medical writings from about 2,500 years ago, describes the symptoms of patients with parasitic worms. In 2017 archeologists were able to confirm worms were present in Hippocrates' time. They found whipworm and roundworm eggs in ancient, decomposed poop!

Liver

Stomach

Gall bladder

The small intestine has three sections: the duodenum, jejunum, and ileum.

In the duodenum, bile from the liver breaks down fats.

Most of the chemical digestion of food happens in the 2.5 m/ 8.2 ft-long jejunum.

In total, the small intestine is about 6 m (20 ft) long.

The large intestine is about 1.5 m (5 ft) long.

The ileum is the longest part of the small intestine. It absorbs bile and returns it to the liver.

The last section of the large intestine—and the whole gut!—is the 12 cm/ 4.7 in-long rectum.

The rectum stores feces until we're able to poop.

DID YOU KNOW? Fiber's an essential part of our diet—but it's indigestible! It helps us to feel full and, most importantly, it bulks out watery waste.

Absorbing Nutrients

This innermost layer of the small intestine's wall, the mucosa, is where nutrients are absorbed.

In the small intestine, enzymes produced by the pancreas and bile released from the gall bladder (see page 80) finish extracting nutrients from the food. They change proteins, fats, and carbohydrates into simple molecules that can pass through the intestine's thin lining.

All About Area

The small intestine is a narrow, folded tube about 6 m (20 ft) in length. Its surface area is made even bigger by finger-like structures called villi on the inner walls. Even smaller projections, called microvilli, stick out from the villi. Having a surface area the size of a tennis court enables the small intestine to absorb nutrients quickly—and in large quantities.

The submucosa has blood vessels and nerves.

This layer of muscle tissue squeezes the food along.

Microvilli cover the surface cells on the villi. Together, they increase the small intestine's surface area for absorption by around 600 times.

VILLUS

THIN EPITHELIUM (LAYER OF SURFACE CELLS)

MICROVILLI

PLASMA MEMBRANE

NUCLEUS

BLOOD CAPILLARY

LYMPHATIC VESSEL

EPITHELIAL CELL

DID YOU KNOW? There are around 200 million microvilli in every 1 sq mm (0.0016 sq in) of small intestine.

Scientist: Paul Langerhans
Breakthrough: Found the cells that secrete insulin
Date: 1869
The story: German biologist Paul Langerhans identified "islands" of clear cells in the pancreas—but their function remained a mystery for more than 50 years. In 1923 Canadian doctor Frederick Banting and Scottish biochemist John Macleod won the Nobel Prize for the discovery of insulin.

This paler area of pancreatic tissue is called an islet of Langerhans. It makes insulin, a hormone which controls the amount of glucose in the blood.

The wrinkly folds on the walls of the small intestine are covered in finger-like projections called villi.

GALL BLADDER

PANCREATIC DUCT

STOMACH

BILE DUCT

PANCREAS

Pancreas Power

When food arrives in the small intestine, the pancreas releases a powerful, enzyme-packed juice directly into the duodenum through the pancreatic duct. The pancreas also secretes hormones that keep our sugar levels steady.

DUODENUM

Tucked into the curve of the duodenum, the pancreas produces enzymes and insulin.

The Liver

No wonder the liver is the heaviest organ! It's our in-built "chemical factory," responsible for more than 500 different functions. One of its jobs is storing, processing, and releasing the nutrients from food—even though it's not directly part of our digestive system.

Hardworking Hepocytes

The liver is made up of lobules, hexagonal groups of cells arranged around a central vein. These cells, called hepocytes, process nutrients, secrete bile (see below), store vitamins and minerals, and break down toxins, such as alcohol.

CENTRAL VEIN FLOWS INTO HEPATIC VEIN

COLUMNS OF HEPATOCYTES

BILE DUCT CARRIES AWAY BILE

HEPATIC VEIN

HEPATIC ARTERY

This cross-section shows the structure of a lobule. The liver contains thousands of these tiny processing units.

Blood is carried from the spleen to the liver along this vein.

Bitter Brew

Bile is a bitter, greenish-brown fluid that digests fats. It travels along the hepatic ducts to be stored in the gall bladder, a pouch below the liver. When food enters the small intestine, the gall bladder squeezes bile into the bile duct, which leads into the duodenum.

This SEM scan magnifies the gall bladder's wrinkled lining. Each bump is an epithelial cell.

The spleen filters old red blood cells from the blood and produces white cells.

BODY
BREAKTHROUGH

Scientist: René Laennec
Breakthrough: Coined the term "cirrhosis"
Date: 1819
The story: Ancient Greek medic Hippocrates described liver damage in the 500s BCE, but French doctor René Laennec came up with the name cirrhosis ("yellowish condition") in 1819 —a damaged liver (left) turns from healthy brown to yellow. One cause of cirrhosis is drinking too much alcohol.

This CT scan shows the liver and spleen.

Three-quarters of the blood in the liver is from the digestive system. Liver cells called hepatocytes remove its nutrients.

The hepatic drains bloc from the li into the infe vena cava, largest vein the body.

The hepatic artery brings oxygenated blood into the liver. It subdivides many times to reach every cell.

This side of the is the larger r lobe. The left o slightly small

DID YOU KNOW? The liver can repair itself and regenerate (grow back). Up to 65 percent of it can be removed and it will regrow in about three months.

Kidneys and Urine

Over a lifetime, we produce about 42,000 l (11,000 gallons) of urine.

Chemical reactions in our body produce waste. For example, when the liver breaks down proteins, a substance called urea is created. Our kidneys get rid of the body's waste as urine.

Inside the Kidneys

The kidney's outer layer, the cortex, has millions of microscopic structures called nephrons. They filter the blood and reabsorb useful substances, such as glucose. The waste (urine) collects in narrow tubes in the kidney's middle layer, the medulla. It travels through the funnel-like renal pelvis and into the ureter (the duct leading to the bladder).

Every nephron has a cluster of capillaries that brings and takes away blood. It also has tubules (microscopic tubes) that absorb substances and form urine.

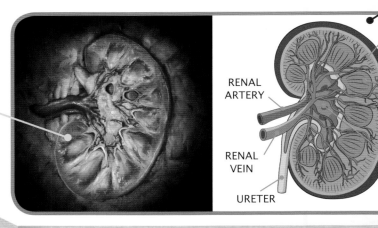

The kidney adjusts the body's water content. If we are dehydrated, the body retains water. We produce only a small amount of concentrated urine.

CORTEX
Contains nephrons

RENAL ARTERY

MEDULLA

RENAL VEIN

RENAL PELVIS

URETER

BODY
BREAKTHROUGH

Scientists: I Fernström and B Johannson
Breakthrough: Found a new way to remove kidney stones
Date: 1976
The story: Substances such as uric acid or calcium can build up in the kidney to form "stones." If they get stuck, they can be painful and cause infection. Surgeons Fernström and Johannson came up with a removal technique that is still used today. They inserted a fine plastic tube through the skin and used it to drain the kidney.

DID YOU KNOW? Urine is 95 percent water. Its other ingredients include urea and salts, such as chloride, sodium, and potassium.

Preparing Pee

The kidneys produce stronger or weaker urine to keep our body fluids in balance. Urine travels along tubes called ureters to a hollow organ called the bladder. We excrete (get rid of) urine through the urethra.

URINARY SYSTEM

1. KIDNEY
2. URETER
3. BLADDER
4. URETHRA

If we drink 2 l (1.8 pt) of fluids a day, we usually produce 800–2,000 ml (25–70 fl oz) of urine.

Rings of muscle called sphincters stop the bladder leaking urine. We relax the sphincters to pee.

Most people urinate six to eight times a day.

Special Diets

Eating depends on our personal taste, family traditions, and local culture, as well as the actions of the digestive system. Local foods and farming have even changed our bodies over time—we have evolved to cope with different diets and process the ingredients that suit the local climate.

Intolerances and Allergies

If we have a food intolerance, we cannot digest that food without pain, bloating, wind, diarrhea, vomiting, rashes, or itching. With a food allergy, the immune system treats the food as a threat. The most severe allergic reaction, anaphylaxis, can cause a drop in blood pressure, difficulty breathing, and even death. Common food allergens are milk, eggs, nuts, seafood, soya, and wheat.

An EpiPen can stop the effects of anaphylaxis. It injects a chemical that reopens the airways.

BODY BREAKTHROUGH

Scientist: Aretaeus of Cappadocia
Breakthrough: Described celiac disease
Date: *c.* 150 CE
The story: Writing in Roman times, Greek doctor Aretaeus was the first to describe celiac disease. He called it *koliakos*, meaning "disease of the abdomen." Celiac disease is an allergic reaction to gluten, a protein found in wheat and other grains. It stops the small intestine from being able to absorb nutrients.

DID YOU KNOW? A genetic mutation that stopped adults being lactose intolerant spread through Europe 7,500 years ago. They could drink milk without feeling ill.

Only about a quarter of all adults worldwide produce lactase—the enzyme we need to digest the lactose in milk.

Fasting

Going without food or drink for a period of time is called fasting. Some illnesses can be treated by fasting. A few doctors say that fasts can have health benefits for everyone. Fasting is also an important ritual in many faiths.

Blowing a horn called the shofar marks the end of Yom Kippur, the holiest day in the Jewish calendar. People mark the day with a 25-hour fast.

In people with a dairy allergy, drinking milk can cause hives (itchy bumps on the skin), vomiting, diarrhea, or even anaphylaxis.

There is less lactose in goat's milk than cow's milk. It can be a good alternative for people with lactose intolerance—but no good for people with a lactose allergy.

In Control

The eight bones that make up the top of the skull surround and defend the delicate brain.

The brain controls our body and our mind. It processes the information we use to think, and sends instructions to the body. An adult brain weighs around 1.4 kg (3 lb), and contains 100 billion neurons. Each neuron can have thousands of connections. This makes the brain one of the most complex structures that we know of in the universe.

Wired Up

The brain receives signals from every part of the body, and sends signals back that tell the body what to do. These "messages" ping through the brain stem, along the spinal cord, spreading out into the body.

Brain stem

The brain stem controls subconscious functions, such as breathing. It connects the brain to the spinal cord.

The brain collects information from the body and—through the eyes and other sense organs—from the world around us.

Scientist: Thomas Willis
Breakthrough: Map of the brain
Date: 1664
The story: Thomas Willis, an academic and doctor in Oxford, England, published a book with more than 200 diagrams of the structure of the brain. It was the first book to use the word "neurology," meaning the science of the nervous system. Willis' names for different areas of the brain are still used today.

Protective Layers

The brain does not touch the skull. It floats in cerebrospinal fluid, a liquid that's rich in oxygen from the bloodstream. Three bag-like membranes hold and cushion the brain—the dura mater, arachnoid mater, and pia mater.

BRAIN LAYERS

1. Skull
2. Dura mater
3. Arachnoid mater
4. Cerebrospinal fluid
5. Pia mater
6. Cerebrum (brain)

In this control room, the computers are tools that the human controller operates. Is our brain like one of these computers? Do we have free will, like the human controller, to decide what our brain does? It's a question that scientists and philosophers have been trying to answer for centuries!

DID YOU KNOW? Just two percent of our body weight, the brain consumes more than 12 percent of our energy needs! It burns about 300 calories a day.

Inside the Brain

The brain's crumpled surface of gray nerve cells is called the cerebral cortex. Beneath it lies a network of white tissue, where connections are made across the brain. In the middle of the brain are the brain stem, which links the brain to the spinal cord; the cerebellum, where movements are processed; and the limbic system, vital in memory functions.

Left and Right

The cerebral cortex is separated into two, a left and a right "side." They connect through a bundle of nerves called the corpus callosum. Each side does different jobs.

Limbic System

The limbic system is positioned in the middle of the brain, near the top of the brain stem. It contains the thalamus and amygdala—parts that scientists believe we need for processing feelings or emotions.

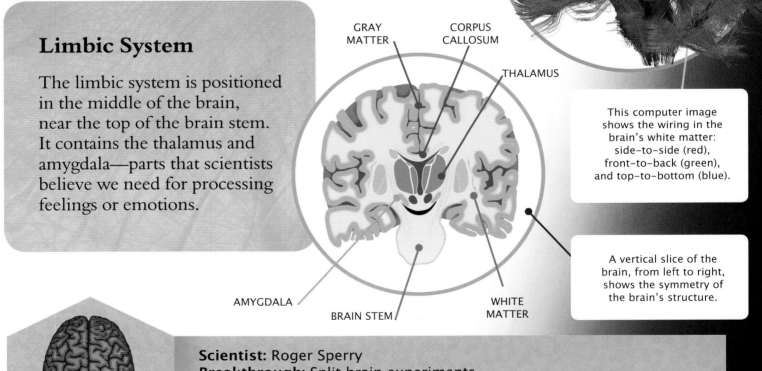

GRAY MATTER

CORPUS CALLOSUM

THALAMUS

AMYGDALA

BRAIN STEM

WHITE MATTER

This computer image shows the wiring in the brain's white matter: side-to-side (red), front-to-back (green), and top-to-bottom (blue).

A vertical slice of the brain, from left to right, shows the symmetry of the brain's structure.

BODY BREAKTHROUGH

Scientist: Roger Sperry
Breakthrough: Split brain experiments
Date: 1981
The story: Some sufferers of epilepsy, a disease that causes dangerous seizures, are cured by surgery that cuts the link between the left and right brain. American brain scientist Roger Sperry invited patients who'd had this surgery to take part in research. He identified "gaps" in their thinking that revealed how the brain's halves work.

This image combines MRI and CT scans of a 35-year-old's head and neck.

Smoothed out flat, the cerebral cortex would cover 2,300 sq cm (356.5 sq in)—about four sheets of printer paper.

Corpus callosum

The thalamus relays signals from the brain stem to the cerebral cortex.

Amygdala

Cerebellum

Brain stem

This bump on the brain stem compares data from each ear, to find the direction a sound came from.

DID YOU KNOW? The brain has no pain receptor nerves, though sometimes it feels like it! Scientists do not fully understand what causes headaches.

Mapping the Brain

Over the last 50 years, we have invented tools to map the living brain. We can now scan and create computer images of brain activity as the brain's owner is thinking and talking. Together with insights from observing animals, these new technologies give us a more detailed understanding of brain function.

Senses and Sensibilities

We have detailed maps of the parts of the brain that handle sense data from the eyes, ears, nose, tongue, and the sensors in our bodies. It is harder to pin down the parts that we use to think—our consciousness.

The primary areas of the cortex detect data—sensory (green) or motor (red and pink). The association areas (purple) make sense of all the data.

This "slice" shows the middle of the brain— the area that's linked to forming memories.

Scientist: Korbinian Brodmann
Breakthrough: Detailed topography (mapping) of the brain
Date: 1909
The story: German neurologist Korbinian Brodmann used new microscope technology and cell-dyeing techniques to identify different tissue types across the cortex, and he related the 52 areas to different functions. The Brodmann areas (left) are still used today to discuss how the brain functions.

BODY
BREAKTHROUGH

DID YOU KNOW? Neurosurgeons use 3D coordinates, called Talairach coordinates, to pinpoint a particular location on their map of the brain.

In an fMRI scan, areas of high activity appear orange or red. Areas with low activity are blue or white.

Technology

Scientists who study brain function are called neuroscientists. They use tools such as fMRI (functional magnetic resonance imaging) to see which part of the brain is busiest when we carry out a task.

MRI scanners can show the brain's structure (an MRI scan) or its activity (an fMRI scan). An fMRI scan measures blood flow or blood oxygen levels.

This "slice" shows the brain's top layer, or cortex. Activity here is linked with conscious thought.

Nerve Cells

Neurons are the building blocks of our brain and nervous system. They work like chips in a computer, collecting a signal from one place and delivering it to another.

Only Connect

The point where one nerve cell passes a signal to another is called a synapse. A neuron may have thousands of them. Some pass a chemical to activate the target neuron. Others pass an electrical signal.

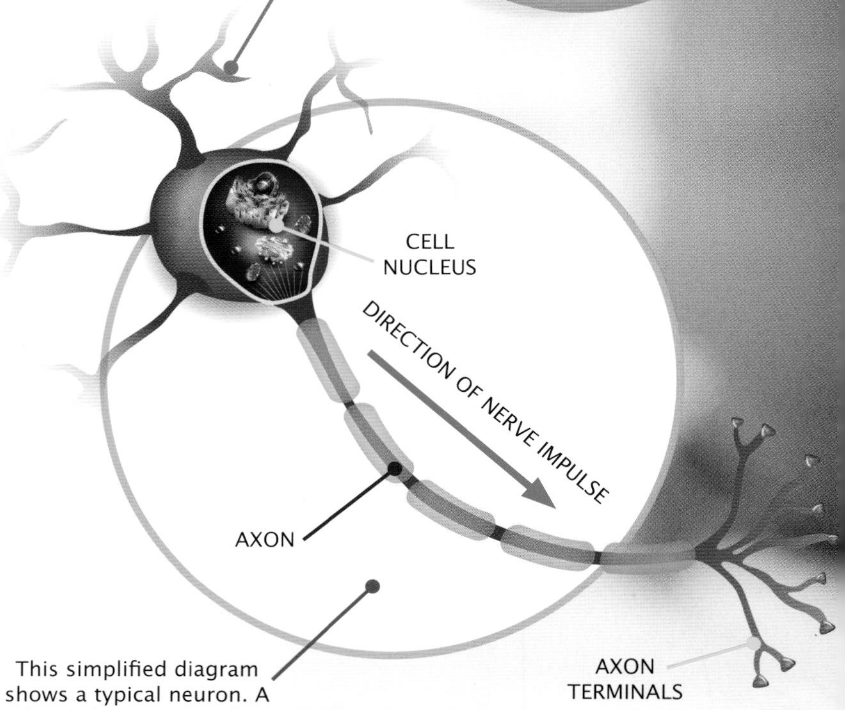

Send and Receive

Neurons have tendrils or "wires" that collect or forward signals. The ones that collect signals are called dendrites. They are always quite short but the neuron has lots of them. The neuron has one long wire, the axon, to fire signals forward. An axon is much thinner than a hair, but can be up to 4 m (13 ft) long.

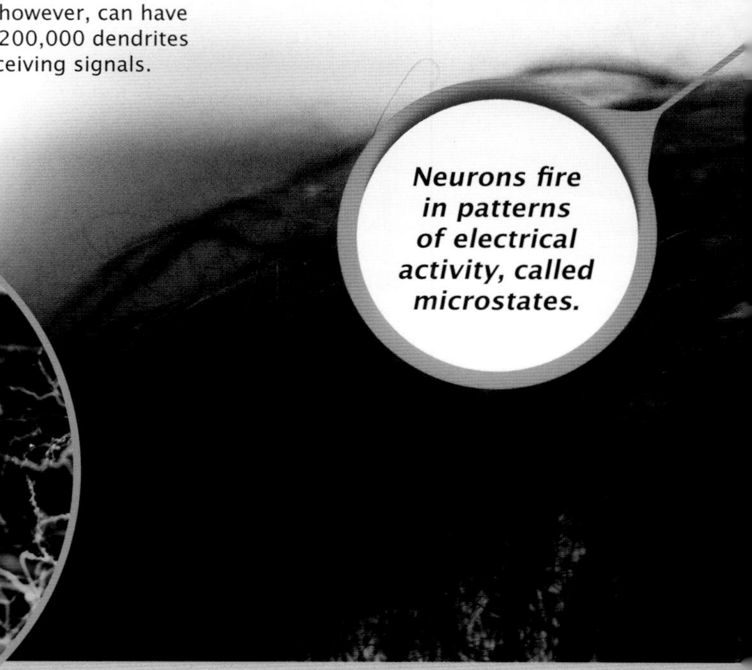

Sensors in this cap detect electrical activity in the cerebral cortex. They are being used to produce an EEG—a recording of brain activity.

DENDRITES

CELL NUCLEUS

DIRECTION OF NERVE IMPULSE

AXON

AXON TERMINALS

This simplified diagram shows a typical neuron. A real one, however, can have 100,000–200,000 dendrites for receiving signals.

Neurons fire in patterns of electrical activity, called microstates.

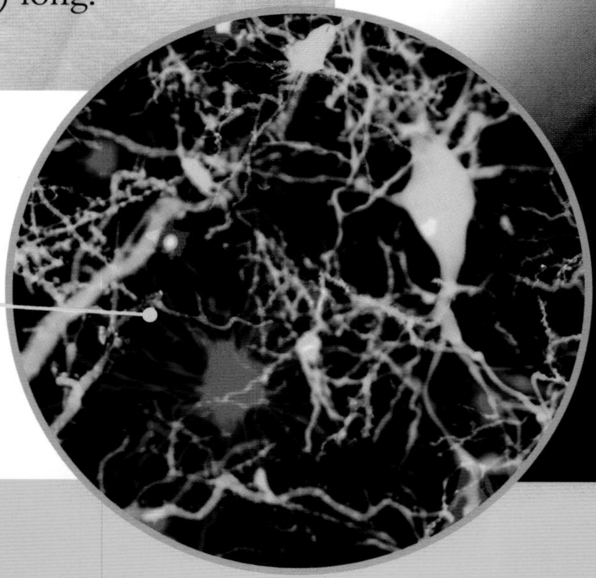

Other cells in the brain tissue support, feed, and insulate the mesh of neurons (green), and destroy pathogens that might cause disease.

This woman is having an EEG or electroencephalogram—the name means "electric brain picture."

Signals from the eye pass along the optic nerve to the back of the brain.

Understanding brain activity may help us manage mental illnesses such as schizophrenia.

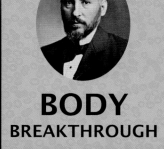

BODY
BREAKTHROUGH

Scientist: Santiago Ramón y Cajal
Breakthrough: Proved that neurons act independently
Date: Nobel Prize, 1906
The story: Spanish doctor Santiago Ramón y Cajal used new cell-staining techniques to examine the tiny synapse connections in nervous tissue. He was able to show that neurons are separate and pass signals in series, rather than being like a continuous wire or pipe that a signal could pass through in one step.

DID YOU KNOW? Some scientists say only one-fifth of brain cells are neurons; others say around half. The rest are glial cells that "glue" the brain together.

The Nervous System

A network of nerves spreads out from the brain and spinal cord to carry signals to and from all parts of the body. The central nervous system (CNS) is the brain and spinal cord. The network of nerves spreading out from the CNS is called the peripheral nervous system (PNS).

Not in Control

Many signals in our nervous system happen without our control. These keep our body systems running—the digestive system processes food, the lungs breathe, and our blood pressure stays steady. The nerves that transmit these automatic signals make up the autonomic nervous system (ANS).

Twelve pairs of cranial nerves carry signals to and from the brain.

The nervous system allows fine control and feedback from the body.

Thirty-one pairs of spinal nerves branch out from the spinal cord.

Running from the lower back to the toes, the sciatic nerve is our longest nerve.

Forty-three pairs of nerves (cranial and spinal) connect the PNS to the CNS. They transmit signals to and from every part of the body.

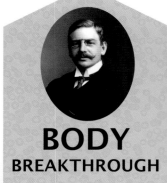

BODY
BREAKTHROUGH

Scientist: Otto Loewi
Breakthrough: Proved that nerves communicate with chemicals
Date: 1921
The story: German chemist Otto Loewi wanted to know if neurons transmit chemical or electrical signals. (Today, we know it's a complex mixture of both!) Loewi electrically stimulated a frog's heart to slow it down. He moved chemicals from it to a second heart, which slowed without electrical stimulus. Loewi had proved the signal was chemical.

DID YOU KNOW? In the early 1970s scientists confirmed that fish and mammals have mixed chemical and electrical synapses.

Nerve cells produce a neurotransmitter called adrenaline when we take part in extreme sports or risky activities. It speeds up our heart rate and heightens our senses.

All parts of the body need to act together to perform difficult or dangerous movements.

A trained cliff-diver uses the CNS and PNS to position his body perfectly. He needs to be able to hit the water safely at high speed.

Model of a serotonin molecule

Signal Senders

Neurotransmitters are chemicals released from the ends of axons, which allow signals to move between neurons. So far, more than 100 types have been found. Some, such as serotonin (found mainly in the CNS and intestines), affect our moods. Doctors can target these chemicals to treat mental illnesses.

Touch

Hot or cold, soft or hard, rough or smooth, itchy or tickly … We feel different sensations thanks to sensors in our skin called touch receptors. We have four types. Touch helps us to understand and interact with what's around us. It also helps us to avoid harm.

Types of Touch Receptor

Mechanoreceptors detect pressure, vibrations, and texture; thermo-receptors sense temperature; nociceptors feel pain; and proprioceptors (see page 104) tell us where our body is in relation to the environment. Our touch sensors send signals to the brain whenever we come into physical contact with something. Our lips and fingertips have the most touch sensors.

Touch receptors help us to work out the size, shape, texture, and temperature of things.

The lips are some of the most sensitve parts of the body.

This model resizes the parts of the body according to how much brain space is used up processing their sensory data.

Our fingertips have up to 100 pressure receptors per 1 cm^3 (0.06 cu in).

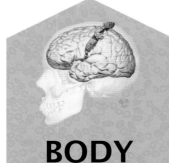

BODY BREAKTHROUGH

Scientist: Wilder Penfield
Breakthrough: Functional anatomy of the brain
Date: 1951
The story: Canadian brain surgeon Wilder Penfield operated on patients under local anesthetic. To limit the risk of harm when removing diseased parts, he used a gentle electric probe to activate brain cells and asked patients what they felt. Penfield used their responses to map the brain, including the somatosensory cortex (left) that processes touch signals.

DID YOU KNOW? A very rare condition, congenital analgesia, means some people feel no pain. It sounds nice, but it puts them in great danger.

Skin sensors in the hands are linked to a large area in the brain's somatosensory cortex.

Feeling Pain

Nociceptors send pain signals to the brain in response to injuries, wounds, or extreme temperatures. Some signals don't even reach the brain. If an immediate reaction is needed to avoid further harm, the spinal cord triggers a reflex arc—we pull away at once.

A graze doesn't put us in immediate danger, so it doesn't trigger a reflex response. The nociceptor signals travel all the way to the brain.

We learn to control how we react to pain when we're children. The sensation can be overwhelming.

Eyes and Sight

The eye is a sensor that detects patterns of light. It turns light into nerve signals using more than 100 million light-sensitive nerve cells. These nerve signals travel along the optic nerve to the brain, where we use them to make a virtual model of the world around us.

Journey Through the Eye

Light enters the eye through a hole called the pupil. The lens and cornea focus light onto tissue at the back of the eye, the retina, which has a layer of light-detecting cells. Rod cells allow vision in dim light and cone cells detect fine detail and hues. The retina also has layers of neurons that send signals to the brain.

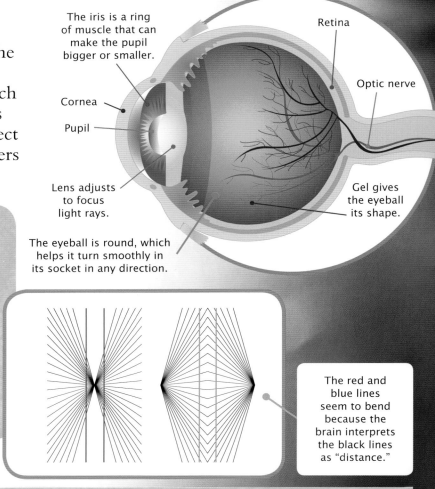

The iris is a ring of muscle that can make the pupil bigger or smaller.

Retina

Optic nerve

Cornea

Pupil

Lens adjusts to focus light rays.

Gel gives the eyeball its shape.

The eyeball is round, which helps it turn smoothly in its socket in any direction.

Visual Tricks

We don't always "see" the world as it actually is. We see what our brain interprets from the data. To make sense of the data quicker, the visual cortex takes shortcuts based on certain rules. However, this can lead to false interpretations or optical illusions.

The red and blue lines seem to bend because the brain interprets the black lines as "distance."

BODY
BREAKTHROUGH

Scientist: Patricia Bath
Breakthrough: Improved cataract surgery
Date: 1981
The story: Ophthalmologist (eye doctor) Patricia Bath cofounded the American Institute for the Prevention of Blindness, which works to wipe out preventable blindness. In 1981 she invented LASERPHACO, a pioneering device and technique for laser cataract surgery. It removes cataracts with a laser, making it easier to insert a new lens and restore people's vision.

Two sets of muscles close or open the iris to shrink or enlarge the pupil. A larger pupil lets in more light.

The white of our eye (the sclera) may have evolved to help us communicate. It makes it easier to follow someone's gaze, because it stands out against the darker iris and black pupil.

Blue irises are caused by scattering light, not by a pigment.

Tears wash across the cornea to keep the eye moist, help wounds heal, and protect against infection.

DID YOU KNOW? One in four of us sneezes in bright sunlight. Our optical nerve is in the same bundle as the nerve that carries sense signals to and from the nose.

Ears and Hearing

Our ears collect sound waves from our surroundings and turn them into nerve signals that travel to the auditory cortex. This part of the brain translates the nerve signals so that we hear noises, speech, or music and can tell if they're quiet or loud, high or low, sweet or harsh.

Inside the Ear

The ear lobe funnels sound waves along the ear canal to a thin layer of tissue called the tympanum (eardrum). Like the skin of a musical drum, the eardrum vibrates. The vibrations pass through three tiny bones, called ossicles. The last of these, the stapes, is attached to a thin layer of tissue called the oval window. From here, the sound vibrations enter the inner ear, which is made up of the snail-shaped, fluid-filled cochlea and the semicircular canals.

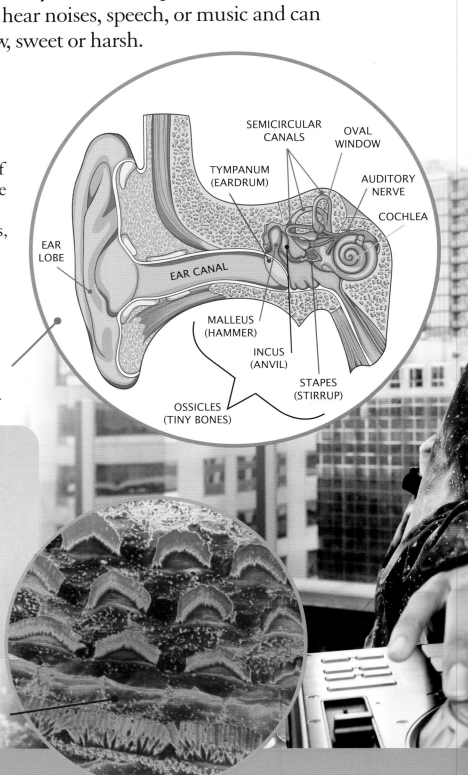

SEMICIRCULAR CANALS

OVAL WINDOW

TYMPANUM (EARDRUM)

AUDITORY NERVE

COCHLEA

EAR LOBE

EAR CANAL

MALLEUS (HAMMER)

INCUS (ANVIL)

STAPES (STIRRUP)

OSSICLES (TINY BONES)

Sound travels as vibrations through the air-filled middle ear and fluid-filled inner ear, where it is turned into electrical signals.

Hairs for Hearing

The organ of Corti, inside the cochlea, contains sound-sensing hairs. They translate the vibrations made by sound waves into electrical impulses and transmit them to the brain along the auditory nerve.

The organ of Corti has up to 20,000 outer hairs arranged in V-shapes in three rows. It also has one row of around 3,500 inner hairs that lead to the auditory nerve.

BODY
BREAKTHROUGH

Scientist: Miller Reese Hutchison
Breakthrough: First electric hearing aid, the Acousticon (left)
Date: 1902
The story: In 1895 US inventor Miller Reese Hutchison designed an early electric hearing aid for a friend, but it was too big to be practical. By 1902 he'd shrunk it down to create a portable hearing aid, the Acousticon. It used a carbon microphone, like the ones used in early telephones, to make sounds louder.

We have auditory areas on both sides of the brain.

Headphones let us listen to sounds privately, without disturbing others. They also block out noise from our environment.

Loudness is measured in decibels (dB). Sounds above 85 dB can permanently damage our hearing.

An adult hears sounds in the 20–20,000 Hz range. We lose our ability to detect higher-pitched sounds with age.

DID YOU KNOW? At just 3 mm (0.12 in) long and 2.5 mm (0.1 in) wide, the stapes is the smallest named bone in the human body.

Smell and Taste

Our primitive ancestors were much more tuned in to smell and taste than we are today. They relied on those senses to find a partner or food to eat, and to avoid fire, dangerous animals, or poisonous foods.

Smelly Science

The smell receptors in our nose detect many different smell molecules, from rose petals to freshly baked cakes, and from sour milk to burning plastic. When smell molecules bind to a receptor, it sends a signal to the olfactory bulb for processing. From here, signals move along the olfactory tract, higher into the brain. Scientists believe there are 10 primary odors. Just like paints, they mix together to make different smells.

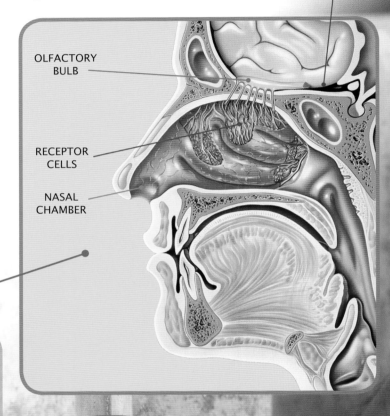

OLFACTORY TRACT

OLFACTORY BULB

RECEPTOR CELLS

NASAL CHAMBER

Smell is the only sense that is "wired in" to the brain. Signals travel directly from the receptor cells to the olfactory bulb.

A Matter of Taste

Taste buds in our mouth, tongue, and throat detect molecules from food and drink and send taste data along nerves to the brain. But our experience of taste isn't based only on taste receptors. Our brain adds in information gathered by our senses of sight and smell. If food looks or smells yucky, it'll taste disgusting to us, too.

This SEM scan shows some of the taste buds on the surface of the tongue. Each one is a cluster of 50 to 75 taste receptors.

102

An expert can tell a lot by smelling three-month-old cheddar ... even what it will taste like as vintage cheddar, in 18 months' time!

Smell and taste data are interpreted by the olfactory bulb, which is part of the limbic system (see page 88).

Smells can trigger memories. Perhaps it's because the olfactory bulb is close to the amygdala (associated with emotion) and hippocampus (associated with memory).

This is a cheese iron, an instrument for taking a sample from a block of cheese.

The nasal cavity contains about 1,000 types of receptor cells. We can distinguish many thousands of different smells.

BODY
BREAKTHROUGH

Scientist: Linda Bartoshuk
Breakthrough: Discovered supertasters
Date: 1991
The story: US psychologist Linda Bartoshuk coined the name "supertasters" for people who experience taste very intensely. She found that about 25 percent of us have more papillae—raised bumps on the tongue that house the taste buds. Some supertasters have to avoid strong bitter or sweet tastes altogether.

DID YOU KNOW? Our nose contains about five million receptor cells, crammed into 10 cm² (1.5 sq in). The average dog has 300 million receptor cells!

Balance and Coordination

We all know about the five senses of touch, sight, hearing, taste, and smell, but what about the others? Our vestibular system—based on information from our inner ear—provides our sense of balance, while proprioception makes our movements coordinated instead of clumsy.

Body Awareness

Proprioception tells us where our body is so we can walk down stairs without a handrail or use a pencil with the right amount of force. It comes from proprioceptors in muscles, joints, tendons, and ligaments all over the body. Our brain constantly combines these proprioceptive signals with vestibular information from the inner ear so we can keep our balance.

Astronauts in space experience weaker gravity than on Earth. They feel unbalanced for a few days until their vestibular system adapts to their new environment. When they return to Earth, they feel disorientated until they readjust again.

BODY BREAKTHROUGH

Scientist: Jean Ayres
Breakthrough: Sensory integration (SI) therapy
Date: 1979
The story: People with sensory processing disorder (SPD) experience sensations too strongly or hardly at all. US occupational therapist Jean Ayres developed a program to treat SPD to help sufferers cope with everyday sensations. Tailor-made sensory activities could calm people with SPD and, in some cases, even "rewire" their brain.

Proprioceptors in the performer's hands and arms tell her how hard to grip the pole.

Sight's important for balance. We stay steadier if we fix our eyes on a spot just in front of us.

The ear's fluid-filled semicircular canals (see page 100) send signals that let the brain know our speed and direction. We need this vestibular information to keep our balance.

The pole spreads out the girl's weight and makes balancing easier. Stretching our arms out to the sides works the same way.

Dizziness

Our inner ear keeps track of our body's movement on different planes (up-and-down, forward-backward, and side-to-side), turns, and rolls. If these vestibular signals don't match what our eyes see, our proprioceptors feel, and our brain expects, we become dizzy.

Our center of gravity is the point where our weight is equal in every plane and we have perfect balance.

Proprioceptors in each foot's 33 joints—as well as its muscles, tendons, and ligaments—feed the brain information about where the performer is in space.

Riders on a rollercoaster experience speed and motion through their vestibular system.

DID YOU KNOW? In 1974, French high-wire artist Philippe Petit walked a wire between New York's Twin Towers, 400 m (1,000 ft) above the ground.

Males and Females

All life forms are able to reproduce. Like many plants and other animals, humans reproduce sexually—a female gamete (sex cell) joins with a male one. Our ability to reproduce "switches on" at puberty (pages 116–117).

Reproductive Systems

Most of the female reproductive system is inside the body. Glands called ovaries store immature female sex cells, or ova (eggs), until they are ready. The male's scrotum and penis are outside the body. The scrotum is a sac that holds two sperm-producing glands called testes. The penis ejaculates semen (sperm and milky fluids) during sexual intercourse.

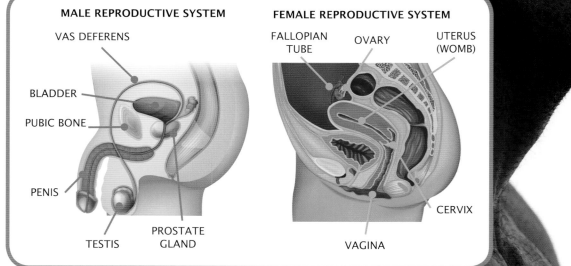

MALE REPRODUCTIVE SYSTEM

VAS DEFERENS

BLADDER

PUBIC BONE

PENIS

TESTIS

PROSTATE GLAND

FEMALE REPRODUCTIVE SYSTEM

FALLOPIAN TUBE

OVARY

UTERUS (WOMB)

CERVIX

VAGINA

Growing facial and other body hair is triggered when a boy or man starts to produce the main male sex hormone, testosterone.

DID YOU KNOW? Worldwide 50.4 percent of the population are men. Latvia is the country with the largest proportion of women (54.1 percent of the population.)

BODY BREAKTHROUGH

Scientist: Harry Benjamin
Breakthrough: Hormone therapy for sex changes
Date: 1948
The story: German-born doctor Harry Benjamin was an expert in people's hormones. He was the first doctor to use hormones to treat transgender people who wanted to change from one sex to another. He prescribed the female hormone estrogen to help patients who had been born male but wanted to be female.

The pituitary gland, at the base of the brain, secretes sex hormones that activate our reproductive systems.

Our gender is about how we think about ourselves, not the body we're born with.

What is Gender?

The hormones we produce and reproductive organs we are born with decide our sex. Gender is not the same—it is about our identity and sexuality. "LGBT" (short for Lesbian, Gay, Bisexual, and Transgender) includes genders that don't fit traditional male and female roles.

US actor Laverne Cox raises awareness of LGBT issues. She was the first openly transgender person to star on the cover of *Time* magazine.

Talking with a higher voice is just one of the effects of the female sex hormone, estrogen.

Life Begins

During her reproductive years, a woman ovulates (releases a ripe egg from an ovary) each month. If the egg is fertilized by a sperm, it forms a zygote. If the zygote attaches itself to the lining of the womb (uterus)—which will contain and nourish it—it will develop into an embryo.

Cell Division

About 30 hours after fertilization, the zygote splits into two identical cells. The cells keep dividing to become a cluster called a morula (Latin for "mulberry.") The morula grows and changes, becoming a blastocyst. Now it is ready to bed into the uterus lining.

Test-Tube Technology

IVF (in vitro fertilization) is when eggs are removed from the ovaries and fertilized by sperm in a laboratory instead. Two to five days later, one or two blastocysts are placed in the mother's uterus to grow and develop.

EGG TO EMBRYO

1. Unfertilized egg
2. Sperm fertilizes egg
3. Zygote (egg fused with sperm)
4. Dividing zygote
5. Two-cell stage
6. Four-cell stage
7. Eight-cell stage
8. Morula (cluster of cells)
9. Blastocyst
10. Embryo (implanted blastocyst)

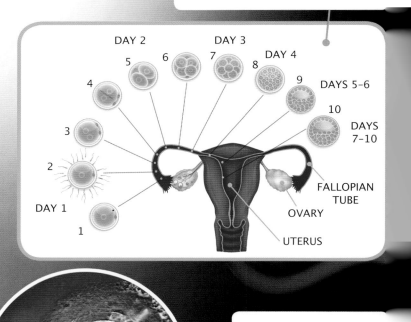

DAY 1, DAY 2, DAY 3, DAY 4, DAYS 5-6, DAYS 7-10

FALLOPIAN TUBE
OVARY
UTERUS

ICSI is a method used in IVF. The sperm is injected directly into the egg using a microneedle (left).

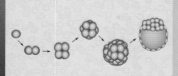

BODY BREAKTHROUGH

Scientist: Jean Purdy
Breakthrough: First embryologist
Date: 1977
The story: Along with gynecologist Patrick Steptoe and biologist Bob Edwards, British nurse Jean Purdy was part of the pioneering team responsible for the first IVF baby, Louise Brown (born on 25 July 1978). Purdy worked in the laboratory, fusing eggs and sperm and growing embryos in controlled conditions, ready to implant into the mother.

The sperm's head contains its DNA. Its whiplike tail helps it to "swim."

This SEM scan shows sperm moving through the uterus. Tufts of tiny hairs called cilia help to waft the sperm on their way.

When a penis ejaculates it releases 40–500 million sperm. Just a few hundred reach the egg.

The egg is the only human cell that we can see with the naked eye. It's the size of a full stop.

DID YOU KNOW? When a baby girl is born, she has around two million follicles—fluid–filled sacs in the ovaries that contain immature eggs.

In the Womb

The journey from the release of a single-celled egg to the birth of a baby takes about 40 weeks. Once the blastocyst is firmly fixed in the wall of the uterus, it develops into an embryo. When all the major organs have formed, it's called a fetus.

Doctors use ultrasound scans to check how the fetus is developing.

In the Womb

The placenta helps fix the fetus to the wall of the uterus, and lets it exchange nutrients with the mother, fight infection, and get rid of waste. The fetus develops in the amniotic sac—which contains amniotic fluid that helps cushion it and exchange nutrients.

WEEKS	4	9	13	18	22	27	31	36	40
MONTHS	1	2	3	4	5	6	7	8	9

SIX WEEKS

The embryo is about the size of a lentil. Its heart has started to beat.

SPINAL CORD

20 WEEKS

Twins and More

Non-identical twins develop if two eggs are fertilized by two different sperm. Identical twins, who share the same genes, develop from one fertilized egg that splits. Twins and multiple births of three or more babies are most likely to be born to older mothers, ones with twins in their family, or ones having IVF (see page 108.)

This ultrasound scan shows twin fetuses developing in their own amniotic sacs. In just one percent of twin pregnancies, the fetuses share a sac.

The eyelids, which formed at around 10 weeks, stay closed until about 28 weeks. After that, they can open, and the fetus can blink.

BODY BREAKTHROUGH

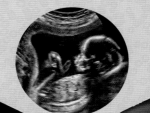

Scientist: Ian Donald and Tom Brown
Breakthrough: Ultrasound scans of developing babies
Date: 1956
The story: The first ultrasound scanner, based on a device used by shipbuilders, was developed by engineer Tom Brown and obstetrician (doctor specializing in pregnancy and birth) Ian Donald. The technique bounces sound waves at the developing baby and builds up a picture from the "echoes"—rather like bats' sonar.

SEVEN WEEKS

TEN WEEKS

The umbilical cord brings oxygen and nutrients from the placenta, and carries away waste.

The fetus's head is much rounder and the fingers and toes have lost their webbing.

26 WEEKS

34 WEEKS

DID YOU KNOW? Born in Liverpool, UK, in 1983, the Walton sextuplets were the world's first surviving multiple birth of six baby girls.

111

Birth and Baby

In the last weeks of the pregnancy, hormones start off gentle squeezes (contractions) of the mother's uterus—practice for the stronger ones that will push the baby out. In most cases the baby's head moves down into the pelvis at this time (about 96 percent of babies are born headfirst.)

Stages of Labor

Birthing is known as labor—because it's hard work! During the first stage, strong contractions of muscles in the uterus pull on its narrow outer end (the cervix) until it's fully open—a process that can take hours or even days. Then comes the second stage, when the baby is pushed down through the cervix and out through the vagina. The third stage is delivering the placenta.

A fetal monitor records the contractions, as well as the baby's heartbeat, which is usually 120–160 beats per minute (bpm).

Babies are born coated with a greasy white substance called vernix. It helped to "waterproof" them in the womb.

The "Apgar" score is a quick check on the baby's health. The midwife marks each of the following 0, 1, or 2 (7 or more is a good score):

Appearance (skin color),
pulse (heart rate),
grimace response (reflexes),
activity (muscle tone), and
respiration (breathing).

FIRST STAGE		SECOND STAGE		THIRD STAGE
	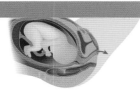			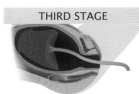
1. The baby's head presses on the softening cervix.	2. The cervix dilates (widens). The amniotic sac ruptures ("waters break.")	3. The cervix dilates till it is about 10 cm (4 in) wide.	4. The baby is pushed out through the vagina.	5. The placenta is pushed out.

The lungs are one of the last organs to finish forming—and the baby only gets to test them with their first breath of air.

Life-Support System

The placenta is a disk-shaped organ, packed with blood vessels. It passes oxygen, nutrients, and antibodies from mother to baby, and processes waste from the baby. The placenta also releases useful hormones.

Shortly after the baby's birth, the mother pushes out the placenta. This triggers her body to start producing milk.

DID YOU KNOW? The placenta forms when the embryo implants—it grows from a few cells that split away and burrow deep into the wall of the uterus.

Childhood Milestones

From birth to three, the brain triples in weight. Mastering a new ability builds fresh neural pathways in the brain.

Human babies are the most helpless in the animal kingdom. As newborns we can't hold up our head or coordinate our movements. Everyone's different, but most of us can sit unsupported and grasp a toy by about six months. Over the coming months, we learn to crawl, walk, and talk.

Great Leaps

In our first year we progress from an all-milk diet to solid foods. Our body grows physically stronger but we develop emotionally, too—we become aware of our own feelings and other people's. By two-and-a-half we are using more than 300 words and can understand about 1,000. With language we can understand more rules and develop our social skills.

A one-year-old can grasp, hold, reach, wave, clap, and pinch. These are called fine motor skills.

In this X-ray, the red areas show adult teeth ready to replace baby teeth. Adult teeth come through from the age of six.

Moving around helps babies and children to gain body awareness and coordination.

BODY BREAKTHROUGH

Scientist: Maria Montessori
Breakthrough: Learning through play
Date: 1912
The story: Believing that traditional education dulled natural curiosity and squashed independence, Italian doctor Maria Montessori came up with a method that encouraged children to learn through play and practical tasks. Pupils explored topics in a "prepared environment"—an orderly classroom space equipped with carefully designed materials.

Going to School

At school we learn to read, write, and count. We also develop other life skills, such as being able to form friendships, and having the discipline to do things even when we don't want to. We meet people from different backgrounds and cultures and learn to respect other viewpoints.

At school we are taught how to work together, or collaborate. Hopefully we develop interests that will continue into adulthood.

Sitting up, pulling up to standing, and "cruising" are all preparations for solo walking. Most of us take our first steps at nine to 12 months.

DID YOU KNOW? There's a theory that a person's adult height is double their height aged two-and-a-half ... but it's not scientifically proven!

Adolescence

The process of turning from a child into an adult is called adolescence. It can start as early as 10 and go on into our 20s, but most changes occur in our teens. Puberty, when the body becomes able to reproduce, is a part of adolescence.

Signs of Puberty

Girls produce the sex hormones estrogen and progesterone. They begin monthly menstruation (having periods) and their breasts, vagina, fallopian tubes, and uterus develop. Boys produce the sex hormone testosterone, which triggers sperm production, broadening of the chest and shoulders, and a deepening of the voice. Both sexes grow body hair.

Hormones released during puberty can make the skin produce too much oily sebum. It clogs pores and causes pimples and acne.

Marking the Moment

Many cultures celebrate the end of childhood with ceremonies or rituals. These help adolescents to focus on their new adult responsibilities, and to build up their strength and resilience.

On the Pacific islands of Vanuatu, boys dive off a 30 m/ 100 ft-tall tower the year they hit puberty.

BODY BREAKTHROUGH

Scientist: Sarah-Jayne Blakemore
Breakthrough: Understanding the teenage brain
Date: 2018
The story: British neuroscientist Sarah-Jayne Blakemore has studied changes to the brain during adolescence. She has shown that rewiring of the brain affects how teenagers behave, interact, and make decisions. It also explains why teenagers often push boundaries, take more risks than adults—and even why they struggle to get up in the morning!

Hormones make moods switch suddenly. It's normal to feel on top of the world one minute, then low the next.

Testosterone bulks out boys' bodies. It also thickens their vocal cords so they vibrate at a lower frequency, which lowers the voice.

In 2015 73 percent of teens (13-17) in the USA had a smartphone. Social media help us connect, but can also expose us to bullying or dangerous situations.

DID YOU KNOW? In 2017 there were 1.8 billion youths aged 10 to 24 in the world—a larger proportion than ever before.

Adulthood

As adults we take on new roles and responsibilities. In some parts of the world, young adults stay in their parents' home or don't leave until they marry. Elsewhere, they move out. Most of us must make money to support ourselves.

There are up to 180 million construction workers worldwide.

How We Work

The work we do determines how much we earn, our status in society, and how we organize our time. The sooner we leave school, the more likely we are to have an unskilled, manual job. Further education costs money, but in return we may end up with a higher salary and—perhaps—a more fulfilling job.

A college degree is not essential for having a successful working life—but it's a huge achievement.

These workers from Bangladesh are in Dubai, in the United Arab Emirates (UAE). They can earn higher wages here and send money home to their families.

BODY BREAKTHROUGH

Scientist: Derk-Jan Dijk, Simon Archer and team, Surrey Sleep Research Unit
Breakthrough: Effects of shift work
Date: 2014
The story: Dijk and Archer studied 22 shift-workers to see why night shifts cause physical and mental health problems. They found that some genes are programmed to work at particular times of the day. Disrupting the body's natural rhythm puts our organs out of synch.

DID YOU KNOW? Around a quarter of people worldwide work in farming.

Time Off

Leisure is the time we're not working or carrying out domestic tasks and duties. We spend it on the things we like doing, such as meeting up with family and friends, taking part in sports, or pursuing hobbies. We also need time to rest and unwind.

Going to the cinema is a popular leisure pursuit, but numbers are falling because of TV on demand.

There are nearly eight million migrant workers in UAE. Most are from India, Bangladesh, or Pakistan.

Construction workers in Dubai work long hours in the glaring sun. Average summer temperatures are around 40 °C (104 °F).

119

Family Life

Some of us are raised by one parent or carer without sisters or brothers. Some of us grow up with lots of siblings in huge extended families, where several generations live together in the same home. There are many different types of family.

Marriage

Not everyone chooses to share their life with one partner. Those that do often make a commitment to each other in front of their family and friends in a wedding or civil partnership ceremony. Some of us have arranged marriages, where older family members select our husband or bride.

Having Children

Some people can't or don't want to have children. For those that do, there are many family set-ups. Children may be raised by foster, adoptive, or step-parents rather than their biological mother and father. Where IVF or surrogacy are involved, children may never know who donated the egg or sperm that gave them half their genes.

A Hindu bride and groom wear red. Every culture and religion has its own wedding traditions.

Grandparents pass on wisdom and memories, and give emotional support. If they can, they may provide childcare and financial help.

Where both partners are male, they can become fathers through adoption or surrogacy, where a woman carries and gives birth to a baby for them.

Family gives us many of our values and beliefs. It's where we form our first relationships with others.

Mothers are getting older. In the United States the average age to have a first child was 21.4 years in 1970; it was 26.3 years by 2014.

BODY
BREAKTHROUGH

Scientist: Margaret Sanger
Breakthrough: Opening the first birth-control clinic
Date: 1916
The story: American nurse and feminist Margaret Sanger saw the health risks of unwanted pregnancies. Contraception was against the law but in her clinic Sanger gave women the diaphragm, a contraceptive device that formed a barrier over the cervix. Sanger was arrested many times until family planning was finally legalized in the United States in 1938.

DID YOU KNOW? Family size varies around the world. On average, Taiwanese mothers have one child, Americans two, and Nigerians six.

Old Age

Humans are the longest lived of land mammals and our average life span (70.5 years worldwide) is still increasing. According to the United Nations old age begins at 65, but experiences and expectations of it are very different around the world. There seems to be truth in the saying "we're only as old as we feel."

Joints can become less mobile with age. The skeleton weakens and we are more likely to break bones if we fall.

Pros and Cons

Decades of damage to the body's cells cause physical aging and makes older people vulnerable to certain diseases. However, research shows that older people are happier and more resilient than younger adults. In many societies they're respected for their wisdom and experience.

Following a healthy lifestyle can slow down the physical effects of aging. This karate master in Okinawa, Japan, is 75 years old.

What Next?

How we approach our death depends on our personality, spiritual beliefs, and culture. To cope with the death of a loved one, we go through a process called grief. Rituals sometimes help with this.

Laying flowers on a gravestone is one way to remember a loved one and come to accept their death.

The pigment cells in our hair follicles die off as we get older. Our hair turns white or gray.

As we age, we may become hard of hearing. We lose sensory cells in the cochlea, and the nerves that carry information to the brain deteriorate. Noise and drugs can damage hearing, too.

Skin loses its stretchiness. It dries out and develops wrinkles. UV from the Sun speeds up the process, so it's important to wear sunscreen.

BODY BREAKTHROUGH

Scientist: John Bischof and team, University of Minnesota
Breakthrough: Successful freezing and rewarming of human tissue
Date: 2017
The story: Biomedical engineer John Bischof developed a revolutionary technique for freezing and rewarming heart valves and blood vessels without damage to the tissue. It's successful on tissue up to 5 cm (2 in), but Bischof hopes to refine the technique so it can be used at a larger scale to preserve hearts, livers, and other transplant organs.

DID YOU KNOW? Japan has the highest life expectancy in the world—in 2017 it was 87 for women and 81 for men.

Living Mindfully

We can make the most of the time that we are alive by looking after our body. It has certain physical requirements, such as air, water, food, and sleep. Just as importantly, we need to look after our mental wellbeing and fulfill our spiritual and emotional needs.

The Good Life

There isn't one single guidebook to meaningful human existence—there are hundreds! In our time on this planet human beings have established multiple religions, philosophies (ways of thinking), and moral frameworks (ways of acting) to live by. Many tell us the same thing—to be selfless and loving, show gratitude, and live in the present moment.

Meditation and yoga allow our minds to go quiet. They may help us to control stress and anxiety.

Self-care helps to improve mental wellbeing but we may need outside help, too. If we have serious worries, we should talk to someone we trust.

Empathy is the ability to feel others' pain or fear. It helps us understand what other people need.

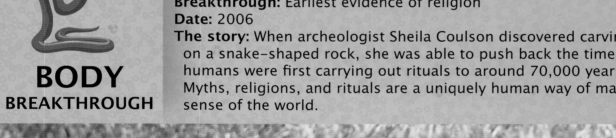

BODY BREAKTHROUGH

Scientist: Sheila Coulson
Breakthrough: Earliest evidence of religion
Date: 2006
The story: When archeologist Sheila Coulson discovered carvings on a snake-shaped rock, she was able to push back the time that humans were first carrying out rituals to around 70,000 years ago. Myths, religions, and rituals are a uniquely human way of making sense of the world.

DID YOU KNOW? Buddhist monks in Tibet meditate for six to eight hours a day.

Past, Present, and Future

It's not healthy to dwell in the past … but it's good to learn from our mistakes. And it's not good to worry excessively about the future … but it's good to have goals and a sense of direction. Being in the present doesn't mean we can ignore our responsibilities.

Our planet is an amazing gift. It's our responsibility to look after it for future generations.

We can't change the past and the future's not here yet. The only moment we can control is right now. By meditating, we can pause and enjoy it.

Glossary

ANATOMY
The scientific study of the structure of the human body.

ARTERY
A blood vessel that carries oxygenated blood from the heart toward the tissues.

ATOM
The smallest unit of an element.

BODY SYSTEM
A group of linked organs and other body structures that work together to do a task, such as digestion.

CARBOHYDRATE
One of a group of substances, which includes glucose, starch, and cellulose, that can be broken down to release energy in the body.

CARDIAC
Relating to the heart.

CARTILAGE
The soft substance that cushions bone ends in joints, and provides flexibility and support.

CELL
The smallest unit of life and basic building block for all living things.

CEREBELLUM
The part of the brain that controls the body's sense of balance and coordination.

CEREBRAL CORTEX
The surface layer of the cerebrum.

CEREBRUM
The largest part of the brain, divided into two hemispheres.

CHROMOSOME
A thread-like structure, composed of DNA, that is found inside the nucleus of most cells. Humans have 46 chromosomes.

COLLAGEN
A tough, fibrous protein that gives strength to tendons and other tissues.

CONSCIOUSNESS
Awareness of one's self and one's surroundings.

CT (computed tomography)
A technique for taking detailed 2D or 3D images of organs, using X-rays fired from many angles.

DIGESTION
The breakdown of molecules in food into simple nutrients that can be absorbed into the bloodstream.

DNA (deoxyribonucleic acid)
A substance with the structure of a double helix that carries genes and is found in the nucleus of cells in all living things.

ELECTRON
A negatively charged, subatomic particle that travels around the nucleus of an atom.

ELEMENT
A substance made entirely from one type of atom.

EMBRYO
The name for the developmental stage of an unborn child that follows fertilization, from approximately two to eight weeks.

ENZYME
A protein that speeds up a chemical reaction.

FECES (POOP)
Solid waste that passes out of the body through the anus.

FERTILIZATION
The joining together of the female (egg) and male (sperm) sex cells to produce a zygote that develops into a new living organism.

FETUS
The name for the developmental stage of an unborn child that follows fertilization and being an embryo, from approximately eight weeks until birth.

GENE
An instruction on a section of a DNA molecule that is needed to make the structures and provide the functions that a living organism requires.

GLAND
An organ that releases a chemical substance, such as hormones, sweat, or semen, into or out of the body.

HORMONE
A chemical messenger made by an endocrine gland that is carried in the bloodstream to its target tissue or organ.

IMMUNE SYSTEM
The system of organs, tissues, and cells that fights off pathogens and toxins, prevents infection, and works to protect the body.

IVF (in vitro fertilization)
A medical technique where the ovum is fertilized by the sperm outside the body in a laboratory, then placed in the woman's uterus.

KERATIN
A tough, waterproof protein found in hair, nails, and the epidermis (upper layer of skin.)

LIGAMENT
A tough strip of tissue that holds bones together in joints.

MEIOSIS
A type of cell division that produces sex cells (eggs or sperm) that contain one set of 23 chromosomes.

MEMBRANE
A thin layer of tissue that covers or lines an external or internal body surface.

MENSTRUATION
The process of having a period—shedding the lining of the uterus if no fertilized egg has embedded there. This happens roughly every 28 days in women from puberty until the age of about 45 to 50.

MINERAL
A naturally occurring chemical, such as calcium or sodium, that is important for a balanced diet.

MITOSIS
A type of cell division used for growth and repair that results in two cells that are identical to each other and the parent cell.

MOLECULE
A chemical unit made up of two or more atoms bonded together.

MRI (magnetic resonance imaging)
A technique for taking images of soft tissues and hard bones, using magnetic fields and radio waves.

MUCUS
A slimy, protective substance secreted by glands and membranes.

NEURON
Also known as a nerve cell, a cell that transmits electrical and chemical signals to and from the brain.

NUCLEUS
The central part of a cell, which contains the chromosomes.

NUTRIENT
A substance used by a living organism to survive, grow, and reproduce.

OLFACTORY
Relating to the sense of smell.

ORGAN
A collection of tissues that carries out a particular job or jobs to help a organism survive.

ORGANELLE
A structure inside a cell that performs a particular job.

PATHOGEN
A disease-causing organism, such as a bacterium, fungus, or virus.

PLASMA
The liquid part of blood and lymph. It is mainly water but also contains antibodies and proteins.

PROTEIN
A molecule made up of amino acids that is a structural component of body tissue.

PULMONARY
Relating to the lungs.

RADIO WAVE
A form of electromagnetic radiation used by MRI scanners.

RECEPTOR
An organ or cell able to respond to light, heat, or other stimuli and send a signal to a sensory nerve.

RESPIRATION
The biochemical process in which the cells of an organism combine oxygen (from ventilation) and glucose, resulting in the release of carbon dioxide, water, and energy.

SEM (scanning electron micrograph)
A photograph produced by a scanning electron microscope that gives a detailed surface view of an object.

TENDON
A strong, connective tissue that connects muscle to bone.

TISSUE
A group of cells with a similar structure and function that work together to do a particular job.

URINE
Liquid waste that passes out of the body through the urethra.

VEIN
A blood vessel that carries deoxygenated blood to the heart from the tissues.

VENTILATION
The physical process of breathing in oxygen and breathing out carbon dioxide.

VERTEBRA (pl: vertebrae)
One of the small, linked bones that form the spine and have a hole through which the spinal cord passes.

VITAMIN
One of a group of substances that are found naturally in many foods, and are necessary in small quantities for normal development, functioning, and health.

Index